John Steinbeck

John Steinbeck

BY CATHERINE REEF

ILLUSTRATED WITH PHOTOGRAPHS

CLARION BOOKS
New York

Clarion Books
a Houghton Mifflin Company imprint
215 Park Avenue South, New York, NY 10003
Copyright © 1996 by Catherine Reef

The text was set in 13.25-point Dante.
Book design by Carol Goldenberg.

www.houghtonmifflinbooks.com

Printed in the USA.

Library of Congress Cataloging-in-Publication Data

Reef, Catherine.
John Steinbeck / by Catherine Reef.
p.   cm.
Includes bibliographical references and index.
Summary: An introduction to the life and most significant
works of American author John Steinbeck.
ISBN: 0-395-71278-5   PA ISBN: 0-618-43244-2
1. Steinbeck, John, 1902–1968—Biography—Juvenile literature.
2. Novelists, American–20th century—Biography—Juvenile literature.
[1. Steinbeck, John, 1902-1968. Authors, American.] I. Title.
PS3557.T3234Z858   1996
813'.52—dc20   95-11500
CIP   AC

VB   10   9   8   7   6   5   4   3   2

FRONTISPIECE: John Steinbeck, Nobel Prize winner.
(Courtesy of the Steinbeck Research Center, San Jose State University.)

For Judy McNee

Contents

John Steinbeck

This penniless family had been living in a squatters' camp near Sacramento, California, for two weeks when photographed by Dorothea Lange in 1936. The father told Lange, "That baby of mine has been sucking sugar and water because I can't get milk for her."

CHAPTER 1

Harvest Gypsies

From far down the road, the collection of cardboard, rags, tin cans, and old cars looked like a city dump. Then the battered bakery truck drew closer, and John Steinbeck could see that the debris at the roadside had not been discarded there, but carefully gathered. The boards, boxes, and scraps had been fashioned into homes.

It was the summer of 1936. Steinbeck had heard about the destitute families camped along California's highways. He had even seen some of the families on the road, as they roamed the state's fertile farming valleys looking for any kind of work. He had seen their rattling vehicles packed with people, mattresses, and cooking pots.

Now Steinbeck had taken to the road himself. He had loaded supplies into the truck, his "old pie wagon." He had set out to meet the migrant families and learn their stories. A best-selling novelist, Steinbeck cared deeply about America's working people. He wrote about farmhands, townspeople, Mexican-Americans, and hoboes—people he had come to know in his native California. His short book *Of Mice and Men*, for example, gave readers a glimpse of life in a ranch bunkhouse. The novel *In Dubious Battle* dealt with striking farm workers. Now Steinbeck planned to write several newspaper articles about the migrants, to inform the public about their plight.

Although millions of Americans suffered hardships during the Great Depression, the years of economic collapse following the stock market crash of 1929, the people Steinbeck sought had it worse than most. Years of drought and failed crops had driven families from their homes in Oklahoma, Arkansas, Texas, and other southwestern states. Portions of those states were known as the Dust Bowl, because of the clouds of fine, bone-dry soil that filled the air whenever the wind picked up.

A dream of steady work in California's promised land had lured people west in great numbers. In California, they had heard, rows of ripening grapes, lettuce, peaches, and oranges stretched for miles. According to rumors, California's growers needed laborers to harvest their crops.

But jobs and good wages eluded most of the migrants. Too many

Migrants from Texas looking for work in California's cotton harvest.

people showed up to pick every crop, and the growers turned hundreds of willing hands away. Fearful that hordes of poor people might settle near their homes, many Californians pushed the migrants from one town to another. They jeered at the newcomers, calling them by the demeaning term "Okies," whether they came from Oklahoma or not. The residents of some towns attacked the migrants and burned their camps.

The migrant men and women took what little work they could find. They struggled to feed their children on the few dollars they earned. They lived in squatters' camps such as this one, and they knew hunger, disease, and despair.

The families paid little attention as the bakery truck pulled off the road and stopped. It looked much like their own dirty jalopies, parked beside their handmade shelters. The tall, muscular, sunburned man who emerged from the truck looked like one of themselves in better days, and not like a famous writer.

John Steinbeck moved among the tents and huts of the squatters' camp and introduced himself to the residents. A shy, private man, he avoided public appearances, interviews, and even telephone calls. He felt comfortable, though, with people who earned their livelihoods from the soil. He conversed easily with the residents of the squatters' camp.

Steinbeck greeted a family that had recently arrived in California. Once this family had owned a farm and raised vegetables, chickens, and pigs. Now they lived in a makeshift house built from cardboard. They swept the dirt floor of their house in an effort to keep it clean and rinsed their soiled garments in a muddy river. They were barely able to buy food, and laundry soap cost more than they could afford.

"The spirit of this family is not quite broken," Steinbeck observed in one of his newspaper articles, "for the children, three of them, still have clothes, and the family possesses three old quilts and a soggy, lumpy mattress."

Steinbeck's bright blue eyes looked into the faces of the mother and father. The writer saw an expression he would see on every adult face in the settlement. It was a look of "absolute terror of the starvation that crowds in against the borders of the camp," he realized. Steinbeck and the parents understood that the first heavy rain would destroy the cardboard house. If no work turned up, the money would run out. In time, this family would be living like its neighbors.

The neighbors slept on an old carpet. Their shelter of tree branches kept out the sun, but not the rain. The neighbor children wore sacks for clothing and were weak from malnutrition. They had gone without milk for two years. Four days earlier, the children's mother had given birth on the dirty carpet. Her baby was stillborn. "After it was born and she had seen that it was dead, the mother rolled over and lay still for two days. She is up today, tottering around," Steinbeck wrote. "She does not wash clothes any more. The drive that makes for cleanliness has been drained out of her and she hasn't the energy."

Steinbeck approached the father of this family, who was once a hardworking farmer. Now the father felt too disheartened to speak. "He will not look directly at you for that requires will, and will needs strength," Steinbeck informed the readers of the *San Francisco News*. "The father is vaguely aware that there is a culture of hookworm in the mud along the river bank. He knows the children will get it on their bare feet. But he hasn't the will nor the energy to resist. Too many things have happened to him."

John Steinbeck returned home and wrote seven news articles about the Dust Bowl migrants, people he called "harvest gypsies." And when he finished, he knew that he needed to write more. He could not get the images of hungry children and exhausted, defeated adults out of his mind. The articles would inform Californians about the problems of the refugees. But a book could bring the migrants' situation to the attention of the world.

The author sat down to write a novel telling the epic story of the Dust Bowl migrants. He turned their struggle into art. The book that resulted from this effort was *The Grapes of Wrath*, published in 1939. It

John Steinbeck in the 1930s.

would prove to be Steinbeck's best-known work, and would link his name permanently with the Great Depression in the minds of many people. It would make the wandering, impoverished Dust Bowl family a symbol of that era.

The novel follows the fictional Joad family, Oklahoma farmers who were uprooted by the depression, as they scramble to survive in California. Steinbeck used the story of the Joads to express his anger at the injustice he saw. It is shameful, he declared, to see children suffering from malnutrition while the groves yield more oranges than the growers can sell profitably. To Steinbeck, this kind of injustice diminished the greatness of the United States of America. "There is a sorrow here that weeping cannot symbolize," he wrote in *The Grapes of Wrath*. "There is a failure here that topples all our success."

The Grapes of Wrath sold many thousands of copies, and it earned its author the Pulitzer Prize for fiction in 1940. It was a hugely popular book, but a controversial one as well. Some readers found events depicted in the book to be shocking. Others labeled Steinbeck a communist, because he showed sympathy for people at the lowest economic level in society. Those who wanted to keep the migrants' problems hidden—the powerful California growers and some businesspeople and politicians—called Steinbeck a liar. *The Grapes of Wrath* was "a black, infernal creation of a twisted, distorted mind," said Representative Lyle Boren, a congressman from Oklahoma.

Senate hearings later showed that Steinbeck's portrait of the Dust Bowl migrants was accurate. And his fans waited for another book like *The Grapes of Wrath*, one that would expose other social problems in America.

Steinbeck was to disappoint the readers who wanted more books like the old ones. To him, the challenge of writing was to try something new. He continually tested his ability. His next project was a book describing a boat trip to the Gulf of California and the marine life he found there. His later novels would be short or long, funny or serious. They would depict happy-go-lucky eccentrics and people wrestling with questions of good and evil. Steinbeck also wrote magazine articles and movie scripts, and he became something of a gypsy himself.

He sailed to Europe and North Africa in 1943, to report on World War II for the *New York Herald Tribune*. He later traveled extensively in Europe and described his experiences in writing. In 1966, he visited South Vietnam and reported on the American war effort there. Many people who admired Steinbeck's championing of the Dust Bowl migrants now criticized his support of America's involvement in the unpopular war in Vietnam.

In 1960, Steinbeck embarked on a road trip to renew his acquaintance with the United States. It was a trip inspired partly by his memories of visiting the migrant camps. He was accompanied on this journey by a poodle named Charley. The book chronicling Steinbeck's trip, *Travels with Charley in Search of America*, was published in 1962. The same year, Steinbeck received the Nobel Prize for Literature, honoring a lifetime of writing.

John Steinbeck experienced life in America from the start of the twentieth century through the turbulent 1960s. He recorded his observations, his enjoyment of life, and his belief in human goodness. His work still attracts new generations of readers. Steinbeck's books differ in content and form, but he wrote them all with a particular goal in mind. As he explained, "My whole work drive has been aimed at making people understand each other."

John Steinbeck and his sister Mary pose outside their house on Central Avenue as their mother watches from the porch.

CHAPTER 2

The Magic

In 1918, the people of Salinas, California, were used to seeing young John Steinbeck sitting at his bedroom window, busily writing. The sixteen-year-old worked at his desk hour after hour. He was crafting stories, stories he mailed to magazines in the hope that they would be published.

Steinbeck later recalled how he waited to see his stories in print. "I would watch the magazines for a certain length of time to see whether they had printed them," he said. "They never did because they couldn't get in touch with me." He had been too shy to provide the publishers with his real name or address.

John Ernst Steinbeck had grown up in the white Victorian house at 132 Central Avenue in Salinas. He was the third of the Steinbecks' four children. His sisters Beth and Esther were much older than John. He would feel closest to Mary, the youngest.

When John Steinbeck was born, on February 27, 1902, Salinas was a town of 2,500 people. Every summer, the townspeople held a rodeo. And on the Fourth of July, the firemen of Salinas and neighboring towns raced their horse-drawn hose carts down the unpaved streets.

The black earth of the surrounding Salinas River Valley nourished many acres of lettuce. A large number of European immigrants had settled in the valley to raise crops and families. "The generations of Portuguese and Swiss and Scandinavians became American so that the

Businessmen parade up Main Street, Salinas, circa 1910.

names of Tavernetti and Sveresky and Anoitzbehere and Nissen no longer sounded foreign to our ears," Steinbeck later noted in an article in *Holiday* magazine.

John's mother, Olive Hamilton Steinbeck, was the daughter of Irish immigrants. It was she who passed on a love of storytelling to her son. Olive liked to tell imaginative tales about ghosts and leprechauns. The stories impressed John so much that as a child, and even as a man, he insisted that he could see supernatural beings from time to time.

Olive had left her parents' ranch at fifteen to train as a teacher. At eighteen, she taught in a one-room school. It was a job that required courage, John Steinbeck explained in his 1952 novel, *East of Eden*. In this book, the author blended true stories about his family with a long fictional tale. "In her school there were pupils older and bigger than she was," he wrote about his mother. "To keep order among the big undisciplined boys without pistol and bull whip was a difficult and dangerous business." Olive taught reading, writing, arithmetic, and music. She also patched up cuts and scrapes. She treated one boy for a rattlesnake bite.

John Steinbeck remembered his mother as energetic and full of fun. He called his father, in contrast, "a singularly silent man." Steinbeck's father, who was also named John, had worked as an accountant and had then opened a feed and grain store. After that business failed, he was appointed treasurer of Monterey County. He would hold that position for the rest of his life.

Olive Hamilton Steinbeck.

*John Steinbeck's father,
who also was named John.*

Steinbeck confided to a journal that his father was "a man intensely disappointed in himself." His father had never felt a driving ambition to be anything great or important. He had chosen a safe, practical course in life, in order to support his family. Yet he would later offer John enormous help in his effort to become a writer. "He admired anyone who laid down his line and followed it undeflected to the end," Steinbeck said.

This quiet man taught his children to grow vegetables and flowers. He took them into the country to learn about nature. John inhaled deeply on these outings. He opened his eyes and he listened, and he formed memories that would last for life. He drew upon those memories in *East of Eden*, which is set in the Salinas Valley.

Steinbeck wrote, "I remember my childhood names for grasses and secret flowers. I remember where a toad may live and what time the

A Steinbeck family picnic. John sits with his father, holding his hat on a pole.

birds awaken in the summer—and what trees and seasons smelled like. . . . The memory of odors is very rich."

John watched sparrows hop along the muddy streets of Salinas when he was young, and he wrote on the sidewalks with juicy berries picked from bushes. The noise of frogs croaking in the swamps outside town lulled him to sleep at night. "I was pretty big before I learned that silence was not made up of a wall of frog song," he remarked in the *Holiday* article.

Steinbeck walked with his father along Main Street in Salinas in April 1906, after an earthquake and fire had destroyed much of the city of San Francisco, some eighty-five miles away. The residents of Salinas had felt the earth tremble, too. John and his father saw bricks that had shaken free from the walls of stores and office buildings and tumbled into the street. The Steinbecks' wooden house had been spared any damage, but the quake had caused the family's phonograph—a prized possession—to fall from a shelf and break.

A major earthquake destroyed much of San Francisco on April 18, 1906.

Books were prized possessions in the Steinbeck home, too. Olive Steinbeck, the former teacher, encouraged John and the girls to read. The children often received books for their birthdays. John read the Bible, the fairy tales of Hans Christian Andersen, and many classic novels and poems. He enjoyed the works of the Scottish writer Robert Louis Stevenson, especially *Travels with a Donkey*, an account of Stevenson's wanderings in France. A donkey named Modestine had carried Stevenson's sleeping bag and supplies as he journeyed.

When John turned nine years old, an aunt gave him a book that would be a lifelong favorite. *Morte d'Arthur*, by Sir Thomas Malory, was a fifteenth-century account of the life of the legendary English ruler King Arthur. According to the ancient yarn, Arthur was born an unknown, and fate made him king. Arthur ruled so well that his empire soon stretched from Ireland to Rome. He was served by an elite brotherhood, the Knights of the Round Table, men who valued justice, bravery, and goodness. The knights journeyed from King Arthur's Court on adventures, such as the search for the Holy Grail. They believed that Christ had used this lost chalice at the Last Supper.

Steinbeck remarked that when he first read *Morte d'Arthur*, "the magic happened." The old story and Malory's words stimulated his mind and stirred his emotions as nothing had done before. He read the book again and again. "This was mine—secretly mine," he said. "I loved the old spelling of the words—and the words no longer used. Perhaps a passionate love for the English language opened to me from this one book."

The Arthurian tales impressed John so much that he acted them out on his pet pony, Jill. With Mary as a companion, he went looking for the Holy Grail. The mountains that border the Salinas Valley formed a backdrop for his play.

Steinbeck wrote lovingly about those mountains in *East of Eden*:

I remember that the Gabilan Mountains to the east of the valley were light gay mountains full of sun and loveliness and a kind of invitation, so that you wanted to climb into the

John and Mary astride their pony, Jill.

warm foothills almost as you want to climb into the lap of a beloved mother. They were beckoning mountains with a brown grass love. The Santa Lucias stood up against the sky to the west and kept the valley from the open sea, and they were dark and brooding—unfriendly and dangerous.

Steinbeck wrote about the flowers and greenery that covered the foothills and valley floor after a rainy winter. There were blue lupines edged in white. There were California poppies of a color that was "not orange, not gold, but if pure gold were liquid and could raise a cream, that golden cream might be like the color of the poppies." The harebells were among John's favorite flowers. They were "tiny lanterns," he wrote, "cream white and almost sinful looking, and these were so rare and magical that a child, finding one, felt singled out and special all day long."

The Steinbecks owned a vacation cottage in Pacific Grove, California, on the rocky coast of Monterey Bay. John and Mary played in the tide pools in summer. They chased each other through the beds of wild, pink-flowering ice plants that grew on the cliffs overlooking the shore. One year, John planted a small pine tree next to the cottage. He grew to love that tree, and he pretended it was his brother.

The hills and the seashore promised adventures in nature. The streets of Salinas offered adventures of a different kind. As adolescence approached, John and his pals amused themselves by getting into mischief. The boys began to smoke secretly. Also, they spied on a man who lived alone and behaved strangely. As an adult, Steinbeck understood that the man was mentally ill. But during childhood, he and his friends were sure that the man was a miser, and that he had stashed gold somewhere in his house.

Day after day, the boys watched the man through his windows. They saw him write in a notebook and make speeches to himself. "If he sat still too long we could stir him up by knocking gently and in a ghostly manner on the wall. He would leap to his feet and deliver great speeches, waving his arms and shaking his fist while his face contorted with emotion and saliva dripped from his mouth," Steinbeck wrote. Looking back on these cruel pranks for *Holiday* magazine, the author quipped, "There was always something to do in Salinas."

Reports of John's misbehavior occasionally reached Olive Steinbeck's ears. At those times she would sigh, "I don't know about John. He'll either be a genius or amount to nothing."

Olive insisted, however, on excellent behavior in school. She knew all of the children's teachers, and would be informed right away if one of her brood acted up. John feared his mother's temper. "When angered she had a terrible eye which could blanch the skin off a bad child as easily as if he were a boiled almond," he wrote in *East of Eden*. John earned good grades at the West End School and, after that, at the town's small high school.

John grew into a tall, lanky teenager who felt self-conscious and shy

A teenager John clowns with his father outside their home.

in groups. He was always tongue-tied around girls. He often stared in a mirror at his large ears and nose. High school, for Steinbeck, was a dull and dismal experience. "I remember how grey and doleful Monday morning was. I could lie and look at it from my bed, through the rusting screen of the upstairs window. It had a quality of grey terror of its own," he wrote in a journal in 1940. "What was to come next I knew—the dark corridors of the school and the desks in the ill-lighted rooms shining fiercely with the grey light from the windows. . . ." He remembered the teachers being more horrified of the students than the students were of them!

One teacher injected some brightness into John's high school career.

His ninth-grade English teacher, Miss Cupp, admired the compositions he wrote. She read his assignments to the class, and she encouraged him to keep writing. John relished Miss Cupp's praise. He was grateful to find something he did well and made up his mind to become a writer. Like Malory and Stevenson, he would create magic with words.

From the moment he made that decision until he left home for college, John spent most of his free time in his room, writing stories. He took long walks in the country to think through his plots. When a story idea kept him awake at night, he snuck out of the house and roamed alone on the dark streets of Salinas.

John liked to use his father's office when business trips took the elder Steinbeck out of town. John would write his stories in the margins of his father's used accounting ledgers. The cloth-covered notebooks

The Salinas High School Track Team. John Steinbeck stands at the far left.

pleased him, because they were easy to carry around. At times, he took a ledger and pen into the woods, where he could sit on a rock and write for hours.

Even as a beginning writer, John Steinbeck paid careful attention to the way words sounded when he strung them together. He read his sentences out loud to anyone who was available. Olive Steinbeck was frequently out of the house, attending club meetings. So John started dropping in on a neighbor, Lucile Gordon Hughes. He followed Mrs. Hughes around and read to her while she did housework. He never asked for an opinion of his writing. The reading helped him hear and evaluate the sound of his words.

Mrs. Hughes was patient with John, but he tended to arrive just as she was preparing dinner. She would listen to him for as long as she could, and then she would ask him to leave.

John was a strong and healthy young man, but in the spring of 1917, when he was fifteen, he came down with pneumonia. The inflammation of the lungs known as pneumonia was often fatal at that time, because antibiotics had not yet been discovered. On their doctor's advice, his parents took him to a ranch in the southern Salinas Valley, where the climate was warmer. They sat at his bedside day and night, and the bills for medicines and treatments mounted. The doctor at last punched a hole in John's rib cage to drain a fluid-filled lung.

Little by little, John's health improved, but he spent nine long weeks in bed. His muscles grew weak, and when he first tried to walk again, pain shot through his body. Steinbeck said, "I fell back in bed crying, 'I can't do it! I can't get up!' " He remembered his mother's reaction so clearly that he was able to describe it in *East of Eden*: "Olive fixed me with her terrible eye. 'Get up!' she said. 'Your father has worked all day and sat up all night. He has gone into debt for you. Now get up!' "

John quickly obeyed. And in a few days, he was begging his mother to let him go hiking in the hills.

That early illness made a deep and lasting impression on John Steinbeck. For the rest of his life, he would have a strong fear of getting sick.

John, Mary, and their parents spend an evening reading in the parlor.

He would take to his bed with every cold, sure that the pneumonia was coming back. And he would hate being near people who were ill.

While John was battling pneumonia, a far greater fight occupied the public's attention. It was World War I. A conflict that began in 1914 between Austria-Hungary and Serbia quickly grew to involve most of Europe. England, France, and their allies were soon fighting the Central Powers—Germany, Austria-Hungary, Turkey, and Bulgaria.

Most Americans favored a neutral policy toward the war. President Woodrow Wilson issued an official proclamation of neutrality at the start of the European conflict and tried to negotiate peace between the warring nations. Then, in January 1917, Germany said that its submarines would attack any ships sailing to Great Britain, including those from the United States. More than two hundred American passengers already had died in attacks on allied vessels. To Wilson, this new announcement from Germany signaled a threat to the freedom of his neutral nation. Wilson stopped working for peace, and on April 6, 1917,

Women in Red Cross uniforms march in Salinas during World War I.

the United States declared war on Germany. American soldiers went off to fight in the trenches of France.

In *East of Eden*, Steinbeck wrote about the war's effects on Salinas, a community thousands of miles from the battlefront. Everyone joined the war effort, Steinbeck wrote:

> The women rolled bandages and wore Red Cross uniforms and thought of themselves as Angels of Mercy. And everybody knitted something for someone. There were wristlets, short tubes of wool to keep the wind from whistling up soldiers' sleeves, and there were knitted helmets with only a hole in front to look out of. These were designed to keep the new tin helmets from freezing to the head.

Boys just a few years older than John enlisted in the military. The high school boys joined an organization known as the Cadets. They wore uniforms to school and learned to handle rifles. But the Cadets had practical duties as well. Many of California's farm laborers had left to fight in the war. The Cadets worked for the local farmers, hoeing fields and picking fruit and vegetables.

John graduated from high school in 1919, the year after the United States and its allies won the war. He entered Stanford University, near San Francisco. Olive Steinbeck kept her fingers crossed about his course of study. She was all for his telling stories at home. But when it came to a career, she hoped John would choose a field in which he could earn a living. She wanted him to become a lawyer.

Her son, however, was still intent on being a writer. Language, with its magic, had caught him in its spell.

Students at Stanford University in the 1920's enjoyed Rough's Day, a time for skits and contests.

CHAPTER 3

A Minstrel

The young men and women who entered Stanford University in the fall of 1919 began a program of study that would earn them a degree, four years later, in their chosen field. One of the new students had a different plan in mind. John Steinbeck quickly decided that a college diploma was of no use to a writer.

So while his fellow students signed up for classes that were required for their degrees, he studied subjects that interested him, or that would aid his writing career. Steinbeck studied literature, history, and classical Greek. He convinced university officials to let him learn human anatomy alongside the medical students. Dissecting cadavers would help him "know more about people," he explained.

He earned mostly B's in the classes he completed, along with a few A's and C's. However, Steinbeck's student records show that his work for some classes was incomplete, and that he withdrew from other courses because he was failing. If he saw no value in a professor's assignments, he had trouble making himself do them.

Steinbeck worked hard, though, for Professor Edith Mirrielees, who taught creative writing. Mirrielees warned her students that a career in writing involved years of hard, solitary work. "Writing can never be more than a lonely business," she stated. "Only by repeated, unaided struggles to shape his unwritten material to his own purpose does a beginner grow into a writer."

Mirrielees taught Steinbeck to write stories that were "true." She did not mean that the events in a story need actually to have happened. Rather, the story and its characters must reflect real human feelings and conflicts. A writer must help readers recognize broad truths about life and human nature.

Professor Mirrielees spent a great deal of time reading John's stories and suggesting ways to improve them. Yet no matter how well he wrote, she never gave him an A. She always believed he could do better.

Many young adults have active social lives during their college years. They attend parties and often join clubs and fraternities or sororities. John Steinbeck, still shy, avoided parties and dances. He joined only one organization, the English Club. At club meetings, he read his stories to the group. He made friends with other students who planned to be writers, including Kate Beswick, an aspiring poet. One club member, Carlton Sheffield, known as "Duke" (or as Steinbeck liked to spell it, "Dook"), would be a lifelong friend and correspondent.

Quiet and serious much of the time, Steinbeck still enjoyed a good prank. Very early one morning, the students on the Stanford campus awoke to hear the bells in the school's chapel playing the drinking song "How Dry I Am." Unable to resist bragging, John told some friends that he was responsible for the joke. The college dean soon learned who was guilty, and John received a stern reprimand.

One of John's escapades occurred in the summer of 1923. Mary Steinbeck had convinced him to take a biology course with her at the Hopkins Marine Station in Pacific Grove. The class needed toads to dissect, and John offered to help. He took Mary and some other students on a nighttime expedition, hunting toads by flashlight. The students gathered toads in sacks, and then transferred them to a dresser in the Steinbecks' cottage.

The next morning, John lugged the dresser into the biology laboratory and proudly opened its drawers. Toads were hopping all over the

The Spreckels Sugar Company.

lab within moments, and students were running and shouting in confusion.

John's parents expected him to help pay for his education, so the
young writer periodically took time off from his studies to earn money.
He worked most often for the Spreckels Sugar Company, a firm that
grew sugar beets and then processed them into refined sugar.

Farming was big business in California. Most farms were large operations, and the farmers hired help to work on their land. Migrant

This bindle stiff spent more than twenty-five years roaming from one job to the next.

laborers—many of whom were immigrants—traveled the length of the state and worked where they were needed.

John befriended the Mexican, Japanese, and Filipino men who toiled at his side. He made the acquaintance of hoboes, or "bindle stiffs," who moved from ranch to ranch. When farm work was slow, these men packed their belongings into bundles, or "bindles," to be carried on their backs. They hitched a ride to the coast in a passing car or freight train, and found work in the sardine canneries of Monterey, California.

The farm laborers put in long hours for low wages. They slept eight to a room in wooden bunkhouses, storing their few belongings on shelves made from apple crates. Steinbeck compared the lives of these men to the comfortable existence of the Californians he had known as a child. He saw inequality in America, and it made him angry.

He showed his anger on a Sunday morning in 1920, when he accompanied his college friend Robert Bennett and Bennett's mother to their church. The minister preached to his middle-class congregation to feed their souls and not to be concerned about their bodies. Steinbeck remembered the farm workers and simply had to interrupt. "Yes," he shouted, "you all look satisfied here, while outside the world begs for a crust of bread or a chance to earn it. Feed the body and the soul will take care of itself!"

Robert Bennett said that his embarrassed mother "looked as though she wanted to crawl into her pocketbook"!

Although working took him away from school for months at a time, Steinbeck never stopped practicing to be a writer. His bosses at the sugar company sometimes chewed him out for writing when he should have been working.

The winter he turned twenty, Steinbeck worked on a dredging crew that was draining some of the swamps outside Salinas. It was an unpleasant job—the men often had to wade waist-deep in the mucky water. But all the time, John observed his co-workers and talked to them, gathering material for his writing.

He also dropped in at roadside hobo camps and informed the men there that he was looking for stories. He would pay anyone who told him a tale he could use in his writing, Steinbeck said.

A young drifter named Frank Kilkenny recounted a story from his own life. When he was fourteen, Kilkenny had walked alone across the state of Oregon. He had entered a canebrake, a tract of land overgrown with very tall reeds and grasses. The canebrake covered several square miles, and Kilkenny, unable to see where he was headed, grew disoriented and lost. He wandered in the grassy jungle for four days, without food or water.

When he at last found his way out, the weak, exhausted boy crawled to a farmhouse and collapsed. The farmer and his wife brought him inside. They put him to bed and offered him nourishment. But Kilkenny could hold nothing in his stomach. He kept drifting into unconsciousness.

The farming couple had a new baby, and the wife's breasts were full of milk. One day, she fed Kilkenny from her breast. His system accepted the human milk, and on that day, his strength started to return. He credited the farmer's wife with saving his life.

Steinbeck paid Frank Kilkenny two dollars. "I can use that," he said, and he tucked the story away in his memory.

By 1925, Steinbeck decided he had spent enough time in school. He felt ready to devote himself to writing. While at Stanford, he had published a poem and two stories in the *Stanford Spectator*, the university's literary magazine. One of the stories poked fun at college life. The other told of a mentally retarded young woman who married a Filipino farm worker. Steinbeck also had written a romantic story about a real person from history, the sixteenth-century Welsh pirate Henry Morgan.

That summer, Steinbeck worked as a hotel maintenance man near Lake Tahoe. Located on the border of California and Nevada, Lake Tahoe today is a popular vacation spot. But in the 1920s, the wooded land around the lake was largely unpopulated.

By November, Steinbeck had saved enough money to move to New York City, the home of many writers and artists. He sailed to New York in a freighter that took him south along the coast of California and Mexico and through the Panama Canal. The ship stopped in Panama City and several Caribbean ports, including Havana, Cuba. Steinbeck had a lively time touring the islands with Mahlon Blaine, a New York artist he met aboard ship.

Manhattan Island in late autumn, cold and gray, contrasted sharply with the warm, colorful tropical ports. In 1953, Steinbeck wrote in the *New York Times Magazine* that when he first saw the city's imposing skyline, "It horrified me. There was something monstrous about it— the tall buildings looming to the sky and the lights shining through the falling snow. I crept ashore—frightened and cold and with a touch of panic in my stomach."

New York City appeared cold and unfriendly to John Steinbeck in 1925.

His sister Beth was now married and living across the East River in Brooklyn, New York. Her husband got John a job on the crew that was building Madison Square Garden, a Manhattan arena for sporting events, shows, and rallies. Steinbeck planned to work at his job during the day and write at night.

Plans, however, do not always work out as people expect. John's job proved to be exhausting. All day long, he pushed a wheelbarrow filled

Coney Island's amusement parks lured New Yorkers seeking daytime and nighttime fun.

with concrete up to the spot where masons were assembling the building's walls. He had to balance the wheelbarrow carefully on a narrow strip of scaffolding far above the floor. Each full wheelbarrow weighed one hundred pounds, and his arms and legs were numb from the effort. He kept telling himself, "Just one more trip," in order to get through the day.

And by the time he staggered back at night to the room he rented in Brooklyn, he had no energy left for writing. His memory of life at that time was a blur of dismal images: "climbing three flights to a room with dirty green walls, falling into bed half-washed . . . a sidewalk that pitched a little as I walked, then the line of barrows again."

John had only been on the job for a few weeks when another worker slipped on the high scaffolding and fell to his death. The accident marked the end of John Steinbeck's career in construction. He collected his pay at the end of that workday and quit.

Steinbeck next worked as a reporter. His uncle Joe Hamilton was an advertising executive with connections in the newspaper business. Hamilton persuaded friends at the *New York American* to hire his nephew. "I didn't know the first thing about being a reporter," Steinbeck admitted in the *New York Times Magazine*. "But for my uncle, I think they would have fired me the first week."

John Steinbeck had found another profession for which he was ill suited. When the editors sent him out to cover a story across the river in Brooklyn or Queens, he tended to get lost. When he did find his way to the scene of a crime or accident, he felt so much sympathy for the victims that he tried to keep their stories out of the newspaper!

Now that he was earning a steady salary, Steinbeck moved into Mahlon Blaine's apartment building in Manhattan, and the two young men explored the city. Steinbeck still had his silly streak—in fact, he would never outgrow it. On a trip to a Coney Island amusement park, he and Blaine saw a cymbal player on an empty stage getting ready for a weekend band concert. They sat down to listen, pretending that the clashing of the cymbals was the most beautiful music they ever had heard. Week after week, they returned to Coney Island to hear the cymbal player practice. If the musician noticed his two fans, he paid them no attention. And each week, as soon as the audience arrived to hear the concert, Steinbeck and Blaine got up from their seats and left.

New York seemed friendly to John Steinbeck at last. He even had a girlfriend, a pretty young woman who danced in a show. And then his luck changed. He was fired from the *American*. His girlfriend left him to marry a banker. She wanted a husband with a stable job and a steady income, she said.

Deeply discouraged, Steinbeck buried himself in his writing. He sent stories to magazines, as he had during high school. Although he now informed the publishers of his correct name and address, he still had no luck getting his work in print.

Mahlon Blaine encouraged his friend to submit his stories to a book publisher. Steinbeck followed this advice. He was overjoyed when an editor at Robert M. McBride and Company, a New York publishing firm, expressed interest in his work. If Steinbeck could write a few more stories, the editor said, his company would publish them as a book.

Steinbeck hurried home and wrote his heart out. Soon he was back at Robert M. McBride and Company with a stack of new stories. There was just one problem, though. The editor who liked Steinbeck's work had left the company. The new editor would not even look at what he had written. There would be no book, the new editor said.

This disappointment was too much for Steinbeck to accept calmly. He lost his temper and shouted threats at the dumbfounded editor. The building's security staff quickly moved to put Steinbeck out on the street. Struggling as he was escorted out of the building, the outraged author left a trail of manuscript pages in the corridors and lobby.

The outburst was an expression more of panic than of anger. Steinbeck later described his troubled mental state at this time. "My friend loaned me a dollar and I bought two loaves of rye bread and a bag of dried herrings and never left my room for a week," he wrote. "I was afraid to go out on the street—actually afraid of traffic—the noise."

It was easy to feel lost in the crowd on the busy streets of Manhattan.

Looking back on his early experiences in Manhattan in a letter to a friend, Steinbeck recalled that he "had a thin, lonely, hungry time of it there. . . . I was scared thoroughly. And I can't forget that scare."

When he learned that he could work on a freighter in exchange for passage back to California, Steinbeck jumped at the chance. And as soon as his ship sailed away from New York, his spirit started to heal. He arrived in California at the start of summer in 1926 feeling healthy and optimistic once more. He took a job as caretaker of a vacation home near Lake Tahoe.

The family that owned the home left in the fall, but they asked their caretaker to stay on through the winter. As someone who wanted time to write, Steinbeck knew he had been offered a golden opportunity. His only responsibilities would be to watch the house, split logs for firewood, and cut blocks of ice for use in the family's icehouse in summer. For most of the time, he would be alone in the caretaker's cabin, cut off from the world by the region's heavy snow.

Steinbeck spent two winters in the tiny, bark-covered cabin, with a pair of Airedales for company. Living on beans and bacon, he filled blank pages with his tiny handwriting. Although only his dogs could hear him, he read his work aloud, listening to its sound. "I put my words down for a matter of memory," Steinbeck said of his approach to writing. "They are more made to be spoken than to be read. I have the instincts of a minstrel rather than those of a scrivener."

He finished writing his first novel in January 1928. In this book, titled *Cup of Gold*, he expanded his story of the pirate Henry Morgan.

Henry Morgan may have grown up in Wales in the 1500s, but he and John Steinbeck had something in common. Both set a course in childhood that they would follow as adults. Steinbeck decided early on to be a writer. Morgan, as Steinbeck portrays him, resolves as a boy that he will sail the oceans and seize riches.

Morgan also has a father like Steinbeck's, a man who has accomplished little and yet takes pride in his son's ambition. Morgan's father asks in the novel, "Why do men like me want sons?" He continues, "It must be because they hope in their poor beaten souls that these new men, who are their blood, will do the things they were not strong enough nor wise enough nor brave enough to do."

Steinbeck shows Henry Morgan turning down many chances for happiness as he seeks wealth and adventure. Morgan leaves behind a girl he loves in Wales. He abandons a Jamaican planter, a man who educates him and offers to make him his heir. Morgan's ambition grows so strong that he even kills his best friend when friendship stands in the way of his success.

The pirate captain Morgan acquires vast treasures at last, including a cup of gold that resembles the Holy Grail. But they bring him no joy.

Morgan is on his deathbed when he comprehends just how empty and wasted his life has been.

In *Cup of Gold*, Steinbeck may have expressed a fear that his own dedication to writing would lead to regrets. Still, whatever the future might bring, he was determined to follow his dream. He sent the handwritten book to his college friend Kate Beswick, who typed it for him. Beswick corrected Steinbeck's spelling and punctuation, and separated his sentences into paragraphs.

Many authors pay careful attention to the small technical details of their writing, such as the placement of commas and periods, but John Steinbeck would always leave those decisions to others. "Why should I bother?" he asked. "There are millions of people who are good stenographers but there aren't so many thousands who can make as nice sounds as I can."

Chinatown, one of San Francisco's most distinctive neighborhoods, in 1932.

CHAPTER 4

The Fireflies of Our Thinking

With his novel finished, John Steinbeck was ready to be among people again. He quit his caretaker job when the snow melted and went to work at a California state fish hatchery. He fed the growing fry, which were being raised to stock streams for fishing. He also conducted tours of the hatchery for visitors.

One July day, two young women arrived to tour the facility. Carol and Idell Henning were sisters who worked in San Francisco. Immediately, John was attracted to tall, brown-haired Carol. She was bright and laughed easily. He took Carol out on a date. And when she went back to San Francisco, he was so upset that he went to bed for several days. He was sick with love, he said.

His boss started keeping an eye on Steinbeck. The new worker seemed preoccupied with writing and love. One day near the end of summer, a state-owned pickup truck was damaged while Steinbeck and another worker were using it. The boss blamed Steinbeck and fired him. John Steinbeck promptly moved to San Francisco, where he could be near Carol.

The people of San Francisco had rebuilt their city after the great earthquake of 1906. Downtown San Francisco had developed into a center of banking and industry. Roofs and streetlamps modeled after pagodas graced the neighborhood known as Chinatown, the section where Chinese immigrants had been settling since the 1850s. Residents and tourists alike rode cable cars up and down the city's steep hills.

On Saturday nights, John walked with Carol along the waterfront. The couple sometimes saw a movie or ate at a low-priced restaurant. For most of the week, John carted loads of jute and hemp at the Bemis Bag Company, where he was employed. As in New York, the hard labor drained all of his energy. He was making no headway in his writing, and he had yet to find a publisher for *Cup of Gold*.

October came, and Steinbeck grew discouraged. He wrote to Kate Beswick that if his writing did not progress by Christmas, he was going to give up. Alarmed by this news, Beswick sent Steinbeck fifty dollars. She believed her friend had talent and wanted him to succeed.

Fifty dollars seems like a small amount of money today, but a dollar went much further in 1928. A brand-new Whippet, which was a make of automobile, could be purchased for $610. A can of vegetable soup cost twelve cents. A tube of toothpaste, priced above two dollars today, sold for thirty-five cents in 1928.

Kate Beswick's gift allowed Steinbeck to quit his job. He moved to his family's cottage in Pacific Grove to cut expenses, and spent all of his time writing. John's father also came to his aid at this time. The elder Steinbeck loaned his son twenty-five dollars a month to live on. John could pay him back later, when he was earning money from his books, his father said.

John worked to polish his writing style. He strove to improve his control of the English language, so that every sentence communicated exactly what he wanted to say in words that were neither difficult nor showy.

He was under real pressure to succeed now. Failure would mean letting down Kate Beswick and his father. It might mean the end of his romance with Carol. He hoped to ask Carol to be his wife. But an unpublished writer with no income would make a bad husband, he thought.

Steinbeck had some good news at the start of 1929. Robert M. McBride and Company, the firm that had put him out on the street, wanted to publish *Cup of Gold*. Mahlon Blaine offered to illustrate the book's cover at no charge, as a gift.

By the time the book was published, in August 1929, John and Carol were engaged. On January 14, 1930, they were married by a judge in Eagle Rock, California, where Dook Sheffield lived. They moved into a run-down bungalow in Eagle Rock because the rent was cheap, and set to work making repairs. They refinished the floor, painted the walls, and planted flowers in the yard. The bungalow soon looked so nice that the landlord asked the newlyweds to move out. He wanted to let his own son live there!

The Steinbecks moved from one low-rent place to another. They lived in one old house that John insisted was haunted. He heard doors slam during the night. He claimed that dishes would fly across the kitchen by themselves and shatter, and that pictures would fall off the walls when no one had touched them.

Even though John now received fifty dollars a month from his father, he and Carol had a tough time making ends meet. Carol looked for a job. She expected to find one easily, because she was a skilled secretary. But she was in for a rude shock. Like millions of other Americans in 1930, Carol Steinbeck discovered that work was not to be had. This was a hard reality of life during the Great Depression.

In the 1920s, while John Steinbeck had been focused on his writing, many Americans had enjoyed a decade of optimism. They wanted to forget that 112,000 American soldiers had died in World War I. They bought cars, radios, and other electrical appliances, often paying for them in monthly installments. Banks sprang up in cities and towns, eager to make loans. In 1900, there were 14,000 state and national banks in the United States. By 1920, there were more than 30,000.

Thousands of people purchased real estate in California or Florida, sight unseen. They expected the value of their land to skyrocket. Men and women invested in the stock market, frequently using money they had not yet earned. They watched the prices of their holdings rise and imagined themselves growing wealthy. Looking back on this era, Steinbeck wrote in *Esquire* magazine, "I remember the drugged and happy faces of people who built paper fortunes on stocks they couldn't possibly have paid for."

By the middle of the decade, there were warning signs that the good times would end. There were more lots for sale in California than people wanted to buy. Such a situation could only cause prices to drop, and some speculators went bankrupt. A hurricane ended the Florida land boom in 1926 by destroying acres of waterfront real estate and killing four hundred people.

By 1929, much of the available capital in the United States—the money used for investment, to spur economic growth—was tied up in the stock market. The prices of stocks reached a level that was dangerously and artificially high. It was only a matter of time until they fell.

The stock market collapsed on October 29 of that year. Investors saw their profits wiped out. Large and small businesses closed their doors

Breadline. *The artist Reginald March captured the nation's mood of fear and despair in his 1929 etching.*

A young man, unemployed, worries about his future on a Washington, D.C., park bench.

in the wake of the stock market crash, putting people out of work. Many of the poorly managed banks folded, and families lost their savings. "People walked about looking as if they'd been slugged," Steinbeck noted. The Great Depression had begun.

John Steinbeck, used to frugal living, was affected less by the depression than most people were. "I had been practicing for the Depression for a long time," he wrote in *Esquire*. He and Carol moved into the Pacific Grove cottage, where they could live rent-free. John built a fireplace in the living room to keep the place warm in winter, and he planted a garden.

"In northern California you can raise vegetables of some kind all year long," he explained. "I never peeled a potato without planting the skins. Kale, lettuce, chard, turnips, carrots and onions rotated in the little garden."

The sea was another source of free food in Pacific Grove. "In the tide pools of the bay, mussels were available and crabs and abalones and that shiny kelp called sea lettuce. With a line and pole, blue cod, rock cod, perch, sea trout, sculpin could be caught." Steinbeck concluded,

"Given the sea a man must be very stupid to starve." Yet there were times when hunger drove him to reach through the grating of a closed produce market to swipe apples and squash.

During the depression, people learned to enjoy themselves without spending money. The Steinbecks often got together with other couples like themselves, young adults with little income who liked to have fun. Together, they played games, read aloud, and listened to records.

"Anything at all was an excuse for a party: all holidays, birthdays called for celebration," John recalled. "Since our clothing was increasingly ratty, it was usually a costume party. The girls wanted to look pretty, and they didn't have the clothes for it. A costume party made all manner of drapes and curtains and tablecloths available." Dinner parties usually featured meals made from hamburger. Steinbeck remembered a dinner party at which someone garnished a meatloaf with strips of bacon. The bacon was made of paper, and had been cut from a photograph in a magazine!

Not all of Steinbeck's memories of this time were pleasant ones. He never forgot how his Airedale Tillie got sick and died because he could not afford a veterinarian.

Through happy times and sad, Steinbeck kept writing. Most days, he followed the same routine. He worked at his desk until he had put down a thousand words in a ledger. Then he tended his garden and walked on the beach. If he had time, he strolled over to Ocean Front Street on the Monterey waterfront, a place also known as Cannery Row.

The canneries that gave the neighborhood its name processed sardines caught by Monterey's fishermen. A colorful group of people worked on Cannery Row, including the bindle stiffs who thumbed a ride into town and the local population known as *paisanos*—people of mixed Mexican, Italian, and Portuguese heritage.

Tucked between the canneries was the laboratory where Steinbeck's new friend, Ed Ricketts, lived and worked. Ricketts had turned a lifelong interest in biology into a career. He sold biological specimens to

The rocky coast of Monterey, California.

college and high school science labs. Ricketts gathered starfish, jellyfish, and other marine creatures, which he preserved and prepared for study. He mounted microorganisms on slides, so that students could view them through microscopes.

Ed Ricketts was a small, bearded man who kept rattlesnakes for pets. He seemed to like and accept everyone. He was knowledgeable and highly intelligent; yet he was friendly with the hoboes on Cannery Row.

Ricketts impressed Steinbeck with his ability to see beauty in all

Ed Ricketts describes the features of a ray to a visitor in his lab.

forms of life—even the lowly hagfish. "Now the hagfish is a most disgusting animal both in appearance and texture," Steinbeck observed in an essay, "About Ed Ricketts," "and some of its habits are nauseating. It is a perfect animal horror. But Ed did not feel this, because the hagfish has certain functions which he found fascinating." In the catalog he sent to his customers, Ricketts wrote, "Available in some quantities, delightful and beautiful hagfish."

Ed Ricketts had a quick and curious mind. He liked to play with ideas, to take a concept and think through all of its implications. Steinbeck recalled many stimulating talks with Ricketts that were triggered by the words, "It might be so!" A whole evening could seem to pass as quickly as a moment, Steinbeck said, "while we pursued the fireflies of our thinking."

His background in biology shaped the way Ricketts viewed the world. Ed noticed that many people assign human motives to the creatures of nature. For example, they might consider a fox preying on a small rabbit to be cruel or cunning. He also saw that people tend to look at the natural world from a *teleological* viewpoint. In other words, they believe that nature has a purpose or goal.

Ricketts preferred to think about nature in a scientific, "nonteleological" way. Values such as good and evil have no place in nonteleological thinking. Creatures behave as they do simply out of a need to survive.

"Non-teleological thinking concerns itself primarily not with what should be, or could be, or might be, but rather with what actually 'is,'" Steinbeck explained in the 1941 book he wrote with Ed Ricketts, *The Sea of Cortez*. Such thinking attempts, he said, to answer the "questions *what* or *how*, instead of *why*."

In some of their liveliest discussions, Steinbeck and Ricketts applied nonteleological thinking to human behavior. This train of thought led Steinbeck to perceive that in a nonteleological world, there could be no "good" people or "bad" people, no heroes or villains. He saw that it was possible to observe people as objectively as a scientist observes animals in the wild.

Steinbeck experimented with these new ideas in a book he was writing, *The Pastures of Heaven*. In this collection of related stories, he wrote about a farming community in an imaginary California valley.

The people of this valley live contented lives, but they are lives built on illusions. In one story, a prominent citizen expects that his son will marry and bring up a family in the house where he himself was raised. In another story, a schoolteacher believes that her father is alive somewhere and prospering, although he was an alcoholic who deserted his family many years earlier. A third story deals with Tularecito, mentally retarded and deformed, who pretends that he is related to gnomes living in the ground. These characters and others are headed for disappointment because they fail to see "what actually 'is.' "

Reality arrives with the Munroes, newcomers to the valley. As the Munroes interact with their neighbors, illusions burst like bubbles and lives are changed. Mae Munroe marries the son of the man with the fine house and convinces him to move to Monterey. And while Mae's father, Bert Munroe, helps the man with some heavy chores, the house accidentally catches fire and burns to the ground. The man is devastated to see his dream of a family dynasty reduced to ashes. On another occasion, Bert Munroe makes an offhand remark about a drunken farmhand who fits the description of the teacher's father. The young schoolteacher flees the valley in a panic, leaving her job and her friends, rather than learn that her image of her father is a fantasy. And when Bert Munroe fills in a hole Tularecito dug while looking for gnomes, the disabled man attacks him with a shovel. Tularecito is placed in an institution as a result of his violent actions.

In keeping with the nonteleological approach, the Munroes are not evil people. In fact, they often act out of kindness. The effects of their interference are unintended, so they cannot be blamed.

The setting of The Pastures of Heaven *resembled a real California valley, Corral de Tierra.*

Steinbeck finished *The Pastures of Heaven* in December 1931. After Carol typed and corrected his work, he mailed it to Mavis McIntosh and Elizabeth Otis, two young women who had formed a literary agency in New York City. Literary agents act on behalf of authors, submitting their manuscripts to publishers and negotiating contracts. Steinbeck learned from the two women on his thirtieth birthday, February 27, 1932, that they had found a publisher for *The Pastures of Heaven*. The book would be on the shelves in bookstores later that year.

John Steinbeck now had one book in print, and soon he would have another. Carol found work from time to time. Yet the couple was still short of money. John and Carol often could not afford gasoline for their old car. The electric company threatened to turn off their power if they did not pay their bill.

A beginning novelist named Martin Bidwell visited the Pacific Grove cottage in the early 1930s to question Steinbeck about writing. Bidwell was ushered into a gloomy living room lit only by candles. He saw books piled on the floor and stacked haphazardly on stained, rain-warped shelves. Cobwebs decorated the corners and ceiling.

Writing in *Prairie Schooner* magazine, Bidwell remembered Steinbeck as "a large, tousle-headed man" wearing a sweatshirt, corduroy trousers, and sneakers. "I noticed how ruddy his face was," Bidwell stated, "that a thin, dark mustache shadowed his upper lip. . . ." Steinbeck's socks had fallen down, and Bidwell saw that "his ankles looked as firm and sculptured as marble. In fact, as John Steinbeck sat in the wicker chair he looked massive and rough all over, like one of Rodin's statues. . . ."

Steinbeck talked to Bidwell about the desire to write. "A man's a writer because there's a craving inside him that makes him write," he said. "A man writes to get at the bottom of some basic fact of life."

The author bemoaned the fact that writing paid so little. "My wife and I live in this house on almost nothing," he told Bidwell. "We never have any money. We can't go out to a dance, or to the theater. But that isn't important. I'm writing as I know I should write. Nothing will ever stop me!"

Bidwell observed that "A disciplined force of will, a tremendous self-confidence, glinted in his eyes. The dim room was too small for such determination."

Life was hard for the Steinbecks, and in the spring of 1933, it became still harder. Olive Steinbeck suffered a massive stroke that left her paralyzed and disoriented. She would die before the year was out. John's sisters, who all had children, were busy with their families. Only John and Carol were free to go to Salinas and help his father care for the ailing woman.

They spent seven to eight hours a day with Olive while she was in the hospital. After she was released, they cared for her at home. John and Carol worked constantly, washing sheets and nightgowns, feeding and bathing the aging woman, and answering her confused questions.

John wrote at the dining room table of his boyhood home, but he frequently had to put down his pencil to answer his mother's calls for assistance. He hated to be near illness, and the sight of his mother lying helpless in bed made him sick to his stomach.

Sitting at Olive's bedside one day, John mused about the events taking place in her body. He noted how each cell in the body has a specific job to do. Together, they enable the body to function. Yet a person, Steinbeck observed, is much more than the sum of his or her cells. A person has ideas, goals, and feelings that the cells cannot know about.

He went on to compare the individual cells to people in a society. He saw that a society, in turn, resembles a great body. He thought about wars, migrations, economic depressions—events that are beyond the scope of individual men and women. The great body, too, seemed to have a mind of its own. He called this body of human beings the phalanx, and he wrote excitedly about his idea to Dook Sheffield.

"The fascinating thing to me is the way the group has a soul, a drive, an intent, an end," Steinbeck wrote, "which in no way resembles the same things possessed by the men who make up the group. These groups have always been considered as individuals multiplied. And they are not so. They are beings in themselves, entities."

Now, when he had time to pursue mental fireflies, he thought about his phalanx theory. He wondered how he could use it in his writing one day.

In spite of the distractions and worries, Steinbeck accomplished a great deal in the months when his mother was ill. He completed a collection of stories called *The Long Valley*, and four stories about a boy on a California ranch that would later be published as *The Red Pony*. Steinbeck also drafted a book featuring the *paisanos* of Monterey. It was a short, humorous novel titled *Tortilla Flat*.

When one publisher after another turned down *Tortilla Flat*, it came as no surprise to Steinbeck. The book's failure seemed like one more piece of bad luck in a very unlucky career. With so few people able to afford books during the depression, the publishers of *Cup of Gold* and *The Pastures of Heaven* had gone out of business. And as if things were not bleak enough, Steinbeck lost the manuscript of his *Red Pony* stories.

He decided to forget about the unpublished *Tortilla Flat* for a while. He began the tedious task of rewriting *The Red Pony*. Steinbeck had chosen his words with enormous care when he first wrote the stories, and those words still lingered in his mind. When he later found the lost manuscript and compared it to the new one, he saw that the two versions differed by only seven words.

CHAPTER 5

Experiments

Late in 1934, John Steinbeck received a letter from Pascal Covici, of the publishing company Covici-Friede. While on a business trip to Chicago, the New York editor had been browsing in a bookstore. He had overheard Ben Abramson, the store owner, urging a customer to buy a book by John Steinbeck. Abramson was amazed that the customer had never heard of this up-and-coming author.

Covici was curious. He had never heard of John Steinbeck either. He questioned Abramson about this author he had recommended, and was handed copies of *Cup of Gold* and *The Pastures of Heaven*.

That night in his hotel room, Covici read through the two books, growing more excited as he turned each page. Here was a writer with potential! Covici began making phone calls in an effort to track down this little-known, talented author. His search led him to the agency of McIntosh and Otis.

Covici's letter to Steinbeck came right to the point. He offered to publish *Tortilla Flat*, which Mavis McIntosh had let him read. What's more, he wanted to reissue the earlier books.

Steinbeck was thrilled by Covici's offer. He received an advance payment of three hundred dollars from Covici-Friede, and he and Carol planned a trip to Mexico.

The trip would have to wait, though, because John's father was unwell. The stress of his wife's illness and death had caused the older man to deteriorate both physically and mentally. John found it painful to watch his father's decline. "Death I can stand," he confided to a friend, "but not this slow torture wherein a good and a strong man tears off little shreds of himself and throws them away."

When his father died in the spring of 1935, Steinbeck reflected on the life that had ended. He wrote to his godmother that he would have preferred to have no funeral service at all for his father. "I can think of nothing for him so eloquent as silence," Steinbeck wrote. "Poor silent man all his life. I feel very badly, not about his death, but about his life, for he told me only a few months ago that he had never done anything he wanted to do."

The sun and color of Mexico soothed John Steinbeck's emotions. He and Carol spent more than three months touring Mexico City, relaxing on a beach at Acapulco, and bargaining with merchants for pottery and serapes. John had planned to write while in Mexico, but the days slipped lazily away, and he accomplished nothing. He grew annoyed with himself and decided to go back to California.

Steinbeck went home reluctantly. While in Mexico, he had received news that would make most writers happy, but that filled him with dread. *Tortilla Flat* had become a best-seller. John Steinbeck would be returning home a famous man.

The long struggle for success was over. Now Steinbeck worried that fame would affect his life and work. He wondered if he would lose his privacy. Steinbeck valued his privacy so much that when Pascal Covici asked for a photograph and biographical information to print on the dust jacket of *Tortilla Flat*, he balked. He hated to have his picture taken. Also, he wanted any publicity to be about his books, and not about himself. "Good writing comes out of an absence of ego," he believed. If he thought too much about his image, his work might suffer.

And would money change the way he lived? Not having to fret about bills would be a relief, but Steinbeck had never wanted to be rich. He liked expensive clothing and fine food as well as the next person. Still, he insisted, "Overalls and carrots do not make me unhappy."

The characters in *Tortilla Flat* also have common tastes. The novel tells of a young *paisano*, Danny, who inherits some property. Danny's friends move into his house on Tortilla Flat, on the outskirts of Monterey, and form a close-knit group. Depression readers found an escape from their financial cares as they read about the simple way of life on Tortilla Flat. Danny and his friends need money only to buy cheap wine. They comb the beach for items to use or sell. They swipe chickens from their prosperous neighbors.

Steinbeck had been picking up stories for years. While writing *Tortilla Flat*, he called to mind tall tales and gossip he had heard from Mexicans on the Spreckels sugar farms and from the *paisanos* on Cannery Row. He turned those stories into the adventures of Danny and his friends.

Tortilla Flat is filled with comedy. For example, Steinbeck relates how Danny's gift of a used vacuum cleaner to a lady friend makes her the envy of her neighbors—even though her house has no electricity and the vacuum cleaner has no motor!

Another episode includes a story about Danny's friend who is nicknamed the Pirate, and how he aids the local dogcatcher. Tall Bob Smith is as successful a dogcatcher as Steinbeck had been a reporter. He can spend an entire afternoon trying to lasso a dog and still fail. Feeling sorry for Tall Bob, the Pirate locks his own dogs in the pound wagon occasionally. That way, passersby may think well of the dogcatcher.

The humor in *Tortilla Flat* could not disguise the fact that Steinbeck had presented the dark side of the friends' lives. Many of their adventures involve heavy drinking, violence, and stealing. Some readers felt mixed emotions when they laughed at these events. They felt like Danny's friend Jesus Maria Corcoran, who says, "When you open your mouth to laugh, something like a hand squeezes your heart."

Steinbeck compared the story of the *paisanos* to the tales of King Arthur he read in his youth. "For Danny's house was not unlike the Round Table," he wrote in the preface to the book, "and Danny's friends were not unlike the knights of it." Tongue in cheek, he said that he was recording true events, "so that in a future time scholars, hearing the legends, may not say as they say of Arthur and of Roland and of Robin Hood—'There was no Danny nor any group of Danny's friends, nor any house.' " Steinbeck insisted, "This history is designed now and ever to keep the sneers from the lips of sour scholars."

As a result of years spent developing his writing skills, Steinbeck was able to describe warmly and vividly the *paisanos* and their world. The reading public savored the pictures and moods he created with words. Readers told each other that they could hardly wait for another funny, well-written book by John Steinbeck. His slim novel delighted so many people that crowds of tourists now fanned through Monterey looking for Tortilla Flat and for the home of the author.

Magazines sent reporters to interview Steinbeck. Guarding his privacy, he insisted they question him only about writing. He blew his stack when one article mentioned his "eyes the blue of the Pacific on a sunny day."

Tortilla Flat won the Gold Medal of the Commonwealth Club of California in 1935, awarded for the best novel written by a Californian. Steinbeck was asked to attend the award luncheon, but he declined to go. Preferring to remain in the background, he explained that the book was being honored, and not its author. He hoped he would receive no more such invitations.

Most critics praised *Tortilla Flat*, but some felt that Steinbeck should have shown disapproval of his characters' negative behavior. "Mr. Steinbeck's attempt to impose a mood of urbane and charming gaiety upon a subject which is perpetually at variance with it is graceful enough, but the odds are against him," wrote a reviewer in *The Nation*.

In his desire for an objective, nonteleological approach, Steinbeck had avoided passing judgment on his characters' actions. Nevertheless, his deep belief in human goodness shines brightly in *Tortilla Flat*, as it does in all of his best work.

Steinbeck's next book would surprise his fans and his critics alike. First, it was not funny. Second, it took a serious look at issues of moral concern. *In Dubious Battle* was a fictional book about a real social problem: strikes among California farm workers.

The state's farm laborers were already working for low wages when the depression began. After 1929, they saw their pay drop steadily. The growers' profits on their crops were falling, so they cut their losses by paying their workers less.

The workers suffered other disadvantages as well. Federal legislation had been passed to aid American labor. But the new laws did nothing to protect the unorganized migrant farmhands. The "crop tramps" enjoyed no right to join a labor union and no right to a minimum wage, as other workers now did.

People with communist sympathies had been working on behalf of American labor for most of the twentieth century. They viewed any dispute between workers and management as part of a larger conflict between the working class and its capitalist exploiters. Most Americans, including John Steinbeck, viewed communism with suspicion. But some men and women had been swept away by idealism following the Russian Revolution in 1917. They saw, in the Soviet system, the promise of a world where work and wealth were shared equally.

Communist organizers came to California in 1932 and formed the Cannery and Agricultural Workers' Industrial Union (CAWIU). Union personnel led the dissatisfied workers in strikes against the large, powerful growers. Most farm workers disagreed with the political ideals of the union leaders, but they were ready and willing to go on strike. "We would have to starve working so we decided to starve striking," one laborer said.

There were 140 strikes on California farms between 1930 and 1939, involving more than 125,000 workers. These strikes could be violent. Anyone who participated risked injury and death. In December 1932, the CAWIU led fruit workers on strike in Vacaville, California. A mob of masked men kidnapped six strike leaders and drove them to a spot twenty miles from town. There, the strike leaders were beaten and had their hair cut off with sheep clippers. The mob poured red paint over

Striking California cotton workers, 1933.

A night meeting of striking farm laborers in Kern County, California,
photographed by Dorothea Lange. Employed by the Farm Security Administration,
a government agency, Lange produced many memorable pictures of migrant
workers in the 1930s.

the strike leaders' bodies, because the color red is associated with communism.

One of the most important strikes took place in 1933, in the town of Pixley, in California's fertile San Joaquin Valley. The workers in Pixley went on strike to protest a drop in their wages for picking cotton. Before the depression, they had earned one dollar for every one hundred pounds of cotton picked. Now, they were earning only forty cents per hundred pounds of cotton. The union demanded a return to the old wage, and pressed the strikers—fifteen thousand in all—to stay off the job until the growers gave in.

The events in Pixley turned bloody when a posse fired on the strikers and killed two men. Three people would be killed and forty-two wounded before the farmhands and growers came to an agreement. They settled on a wage of seventy-five cents per hundred pounds for picking cotton.

Three thousand people attended the funeral for the men who had been killed. Eight of the gunmen who fired on the people at Pixley were arrested and tried. But a jury acquitted them, insisting that the gunmen were fighting communism and had acted out of patriotism.

Judges, police officers, and local citizens always sided with the growers in the labor disputes. One sheriff's deputy summed up the prevailing opinion this way: "We protect our farmers. . . . They are our best people. They are always with us. They keep the county going. They put us in here and they can put us out again, so we serve them."

The growers got together and formed their own organization, the Associated Farmers of California, Inc. The Associated Farmers, whose membership would reach forty thousand, controlled the California Cavaliers, an armed vigilante group dedicated to quashing "all un-American activity among farm labor." Its members burned crosses near the camps where laborers slept and terrorized the workers in other ways. But the strikes continued.

In the spring of 1934, an acquaintance named Sis Reamer took John Steinbeck to Seaside, California, and into the attic of a farmhouse.

There she introduced him to two men using assumed names—Carl Williams and Cecil McKiddy. The men had organized a strike in the San Joaquin Valley and were now in hiding, fearing for their safety. Sis Reamer hoped Steinbeck would use his writing skills to publicize the strikers' problems.

Steinbeck was always interested in a good story. Knowing the men needed money, he paid them to tell of their experiences. He went to the camps where the farm workers stayed and asked about their lives. The laborers told him they earned enough money to buy a little food, and nothing else. Sometimes, they were paid in tokens that could be spent only at a company store. They worked season after season, the farmhands said, and had nothing to show for it.

Children pump water at a camp for migrant cotton workers.

The novelist learned how the Associated Farmers made life even harder for the workers who went on strike. Normally, migrant workers and their families lived in camps operated by their employers. Now the growers kicked the striking workers off of their property. The strikers set up their own camps, often on land donated by sympathetic people.

Still, the growers would not leave them alone. Claiming to be concerned about the workers' health, the growers pressured local officials to require improved sanitation in the new camps. The workers needed garbage cans, water pipes, and flushing toilets, the Associated Farmers said. The growers failed to mention that those amenities were often missing from their own camps.

Steinbeck found in this conflict the raw material for a novel. He talked with Cecil McKiddy some more, and he met with other strike leaders. On farms and at roadside camps, he listened carefully to how the crop tramps spoke. He wanted to capture their language on paper—profanity, bad grammar, and all. He was sick of books that presented "the noble working man talking very like a junior college professor," he said. His characters would be real people who cursed and argued and spat on the ground.

In Dubious Battle describes a strike by apple pickers in a fictional California valley. Steinbeck borrowed details from several real strikes and wove them into his story. "The book is brutal," he explained. "I wanted to be merely a recording consciousness, judging nothing, simply putting down the thing."

Not only did Steinbeck use a nonteleological approach, but he presented the striking workers as an example of the phalanx, the great body of people. One of the characters in the book states, "I want to watch these group-men, for they seem to me to be a new individual, not at all like single men. A man in a group isn't himself at all: he's a cell in an organism that isn't like him any more than the cells in your body are like you."

No one knew in 1935 how the labor strife would end, and Steinbeck did not want his book to contain events that history would later show to be false. He wanted to present this story as one episode in humanity's long, continuing history. "I tried to indicate this by stopping on a high point, leaving out any conclusion," he said. Experimenting with the form of the novel, Steinbeck ended the book very abruptly—with an unfinished sentence.

In Dubious Battle came out in January 1936, and it was well received. Most objections to the book were political. Communists grumbled that the strike leaders in the book seemed ruthless. Other people said Steinbeck's portrait of the communists was too sympathetic. The author complained to Mavis McIntosh that "neither side is willing to suspect that the communist is a human, subject to the weaknesses of humans and to the greatnesses of humans."

The Steinbecks now had enough money to build a house in the quiet,

Carol Steinbeck.

forested hills near Los Gatos, California, an hour's drive north of Monterey. John worried that his growing reputation would intrude on his freedom to do and say what he wished, and to write whatever he chose. He comforted himself with the thought that his fame would be short-lived. Soon, he told himself, interest in his books would die out, and the public would forget his name.

In order to make that happen, he started work on a pessimistic little book, one that was sure to appeal to a small reading audience. That book would be titled *Of Mice and Men*, and it would turn out to be his most popular one yet!

The book focuses on a small cast of characters. Steinbeck returned to the years before the depression to write about George Milton and Lennie Small, a pair of bindle stiffs traveling together.

Wiry little George looks after the huge, slow-witted Lennie. The two men share a dream that one day, they will stop traveling, buy a farm of their own, *"an' live off the fatta the lan'."* Like all human beings, they dream of a perfect life.

Lennie is attracted to soft textures, to the fuzz of puppies and the silk of women's dresses. For him, having furry rabbits to tend is an important part of the dream.

"Hell of a nice fella, but he ain't bright," is how George describes Lennie to the other men working at a ranch near Soledad, California. He conceals the fact that Lennie can be dangerous. With his brute strength, Lennie destroys the small animals he picks up to pet. He and George fled their last job after Lennie was accused of attacking a woman.

Lennie quickly runs into trouble at the new ranch. The boss's pugnacious son, Curley, picks a fight with him and winds up with a crushed hand. Curley's bride, bored on the ranch, strikes up a conversation with Lennie. She panics when he strokes her soft hair, and screams as she tries to get away from him.

"Please don't do that. George'll be mad," Lennie yells. He shakes the

Actors Broderick Crawford and Claire Luce portray Lennie Small and Curley's wife in Of Mice and Men *on Broadway, 1937. (Courtesy of the Steinbeck Research Center, San Jose State University)*

young woman to silence her. He shakes her so violently that he breaks her neck.

George now understands that being responsible for Lennie means protecting other people from his bearish strength. George finally shoots Lennie in the back of the head, as if he were an old and useless dog. The dream of the farm and rabbits dies as well. Like all human dreams of perfection, it never would have been realized, even if Lennie had lived.

This new book had been another experiment for John Steinbeck. He had tried to write a novel that was very much like a play. "I constructed it in scenes and filled in the character descriptions and painted in the background," he explained in an interview published in the *New York Times* in 1937. Most of the story is told in dialogue. The action takes place in a few locations and in a short time span, just as it would if the story were acted out on a stage.

Steinbeck was writing during a time of great experimentation in American fiction. In 1925, John Dos Passos had published *Manhattan Transfer*, his first novel to employ song lyrics, news headlines, and facts about real people in telling a story.

Ernest Hemingway created a sensation with such books as *The Sun Also Rises* (1926) and *A Farewell to Arms* (1929). Hemingway pioneered a crisp, simple writing style. Readers had to figure out his characters' thoughts and feelings from Hemingway's descriptions of their actions.

The southern writer William Faulkner experimented with long, convoluted sentences and multiple narrators in *The Sound and the Fury* (1929) and other books. Faulkner was interested in stream-of-consciousness writing—recording a character's thoughts as they occurred in the mind, one after another.

By May 1936, John Steinbeck had just about finished *Of Mice and Men*. He and Carol went out one night and left their new setter pup, Toby, home alone. Toby was teething, and John and Carol came home to find that the puppy had chewed half of the manuscript to shreds. Toby escaped punishment from his angry owners. John "didn't want to ruin a good dog for a [manuscript] I'm not sure is good at all," he wrote to Elizabeth Otis.

John rewrote the lost pages. And by mid-August, when the book was finished, he was already planning his next project. George West, an editor with the *San Francisco News*, wanted a series of articles on a new group of migrant workers for his paper. He asked John Steinbeck to take on the assignment.

Traveling on the wind at thirty miles per hour, a dust cloud rolls over Prowers County, Colorado.

CHAPTER 6

A Truly American Book

The depression hit hard in Oklahoma, east Texas, and Arkansas. This was a region of small farms, where family members worked together to raise cotton, wheat, and corn. Some families owned the soil they plowed. Some were tenant farmers, working fields owned by others.

Like the California growers, the small farmers of the Southwest saw their earnings drop sharply in the early 1930s. Many mortgaged their land to get money to meet their expenses.

The government tried to help the nation's farmers by paying subsidies to those who took their land out of production. With less produce available, it was hoped that prices would rise. Millions of acres were left fallow, and thousands of tenant farmers found themselves evicted. They hopped on buses or trains, or packed their belongings into cars and trucks and took to the highway. They headed for the industrial cities of the North, or they traveled west on Route 66 to California.

Movies had shown California to be a land of palm trees and luxury. California was "where the sun always shines," according to a folk song. It was a "poor man's heaven."

Drought sent another group of migrants west. A devastating drought parched the Great Plains during the depression. Some areas had no rain at all in 1934 and again in 1936. Cotton plants shriveled and died. With

Drought refugees from Abilene, Texas. The father of this family said to Dorothea Lange, "The finest people in the world, live in Texas, but I just can't seem to accomplish nothin' there. Two year drought then a crop, then two years drought and so on."

no crops to sell, farmers could not make their mortgage payments and lost their land. They joined the exodus.

In the panhandles of Texas and Oklahoma, in parts of New Mexico, Colorado, and Kansas, relentless winds raised clouds of dusty soil. The dust suffocated livestock. It worked its way into barns and houses. It settled on roads and along fences like snowdrifts. Nothing could grow

The pile of dust on this Cimarron County, Oklahoma, farm looked like a desert sand dune.

in the thirsty earth of the Dust Bowl. Many more families grew discouraged and took to the road.

More than 300,000 southwestern migrants arrived in California in the 1930s. These were the people Steinbeck would write about.

The newcomers were amazed by the huge farming operations they saw. California agriculture looked nothing like the family farms they were used to. "Where are the farmers?" one man asked. "Where are the farmhouses?"

A farmer clears drifts of soil from a highway near Guymon, Oklahoma.

The influx of people from the Southwest overwhelmed California's agricultural industry. The people of the Dust Bowl competed with the rest of the migrant labor force for any available jobs. Distrustful of unions, they shied away from strikes. Sometimes they worked as scabs, taking the strikers' jobs in the fields.

Often, though, the southwesterners roamed from place to place, unable to find work. Native Californians feared that the "Okies" and "Arkies" would bring slums and diseases to their towns. They looked

A family from Tulsa, Oklahoma, stops for lunch beside a highway in Fresno, California.

with alarm at the "Little Oklahomas," the collections of shacks outside their communities where southwesterners lived. The sight of hungry, destitute people was even more common in winter, when there was no work on the farms. In Bakersfield, Fresno, and elsewhere, residents taunted the migrants and forced them to move on.

A small number of the migrants found a refuge from squalor in the new government sanitary camps. Federal authorities had established several model camps for the migrant workers that offered clean tents and cabins, running water, and medical care. George West of the *San Francisco News* advised Steinbeck to visit one of those camps.

Wanting to attract little notice as he traveled among the southwesterners, Steinbeck bought a beat-up old bakery truck. He outfitted it with cooking and camping supplies. He drove to the Arvin Sanitary Camp, a government facility near Bakersfield, California. It was a place the migrants called Weedpatch.

The Arvin Sanitary Camp.

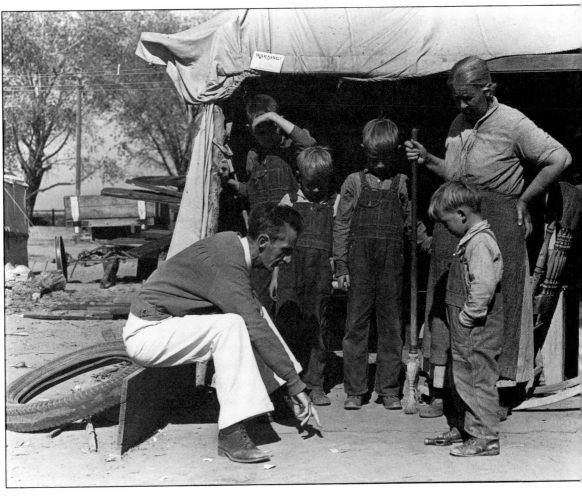

Tom Collins chats with a migrant woman and her four sons.

Rain was falling when Steinbeck pulled into the government camp. He rolled past rows of tents and came to a stop. He soon found the camp office, where he joined a crowd of rain-soaked men and women standing around the desk of Tom Collins, the camp manager.

Collins was a short, slight man wearing a threadbare white suit. "He had a small moustache," Steinbeck observed. "His graying black hair stood up on his head like the quills of a frightened porcupine." Collins's eyes showed that he was "tired beyond sleepiness," Steinbeck wrote, "the kind of tired that won't let you sleep even if you have time and a bed."

Immediately, Collins impressed the writer with his skill in working with the migrants. He answered questions, settled disputes, and found space for children with measles in a quarantine tent. "Tom Collins trotted back and forth explaining, coaxing, now and then threatening, trying to keep the peace," Steinbeck noted.

As busy as he was, Collins made time to show his visitor around the camp. He introduced Steinbeck to migrant families and brought him to committee meetings. Many residents of Weedpatch served on committees that oversaw the day-to-day operation of the camp. Collins gave Steinbeck copies of his camp reports, which contained a great deal of information about migrant life.

Collins had recorded many happenings at Weedpatch in his reports. For example, he described a meeting at which two migrant women discussed ways to conserve toilet paper in the "sanitary unit," or rest room. "One suggested sprinkling red pepper through the roll," Collins wrote. "The other suggested a wire be attached to the roll so that every time a sheet was torn off the big bell placed on the outside of the building for the purpose would ring and let everyone know who was in the sanitary unit and what she was doing." Collins added that neither idea was tried.

Collins was pleased that Steinbeck planned to write about Weedpatch for the newspaper, but he urged the author to see another side of migrant life before heading home. He suggested that Steinbeck stop at one of the squatters' camps, where survival was a daily effort.

Steinbeck followed Collins's advice and came face to face with hardship he never could have imagined. He saw families too poor to buy food, people drinking from dirty irrigation ditches, and diseased and dying children.

A girl watches her mother wash clothes at the Tulare Government Camp in Visalia, California.

This man at the Tulare Government Camp decided to pack up his belongings and return to Oklahoma.

A squatters' camp like many in California.

Harvesting lettuce in Salinas during peaceful times.

Sheriff's deputies armed with clubs guard the entrance to a Salinas lettuce field.

Steinbeck was a highly sensitive man. He reacted so strongly to what he saw that his emotions felt like physical pain. He told Tom Collins, "Something hit me and hit me hard for it hurts inside clear to the back of my head." Memories of the squatters' camp would haunt him for months.

The articles on the southwestern migrants appeared in the *San Francisco News* in October 1936. They informed stunned readers about the misery that existed just outside their own communities. But Steinbeck could not clear the painful images from his mind. Every time he thought about the hopelessness in the squatters' camp, he felt sorrow, anger, and frustration. He sent a check to Tom Collins to buy some pigs for Weedpatch. He wished he could do more.

And then something happened that upset John Steinbeck even further. The lettuce workers in Salinas went on strike, and violence broke out in his hometown.

The Salinas Valley produced most of the lettuce consumed in the United States. Migrant laborers harvested the heads of lettuce in the fields and packed them in crates for shipping throughout the country. The lettuce workers had formed a union, and late in 1936, three thousand packinghouse employees and five hundred lettuce pickers went on strike.

Once more, the police sided with the landowners. The police swore in twenty-five hundred citizens as deputies. Anyone who did not own a shotgun or rifle was given an ax handle to use as a weapon. The "Citizens' Army" patrolled the streets, attacking the strikers and destroying their camps. The armed men and boys threatened to lynch any reporters and photographers who "didn't get the hell out of Salinas."

The community succeeded in crushing the strike. The lettuce growers strung barbed wire around the packinghouses and stationed armed guards on the roofs. They brought in scabs to pack the lettuce for shipment.

Steinbeck started to write a biting, satirical book about a farm labor dispute in a town much like Salinas. He called the book *L'Affaire Lettuceberg*. Venting his strong emotions, he portrayed the growers and townspeople as cruel buffoons.

It felt good to get the anger out of his system, but Steinbeck was dissatisfied with the result. The book did not do justice to its important subject. It was a "smart-alec book," he said. Steinbeck saw that he had failed in his effort to help people understand one another. He destroyed the manuscript and started fresh. He resolved to write about the southwestern migrants, and to do so with depth and dignity.

Needing to know more about his subject, he returned to the migrants' world in the fall of 1937. He worked beside the people in the fields and slept in their squatters' camps. He kept his identity a secret, because the Associated Farmers were already angry at him for exposing their tactics. Steinbeck knew they would not hesitate to use violence against him if they found out what he was up to.

John Steinbeck made a third trip to the San Joaquin Valley in February 1938, after heavy rains flooded the region. The squatters' camps turned to mud, and the impoverished families were stranded. For ten days, Steinbeck worked with Tom Collins, doing whatever he could to help the wet, hungry, and sick people.

The two men waded through mud to pull adults and children from waterlogged tents. They barely had time to eat. Once, they dropped, exhausted, in a slushy field to grab a few hours of rest. Collins awoke to find John still asleep. "He was a mass of mud and slime," Collins recalled. "His face was a mucky mask punctuated with eyes, a nose and a mouth."

The men found one woman who was nearly dead from starvation. She had given any food she had to her young ones. Steinbeck trudged to the nearest store, two miles away, to buy this family something to eat.

Public health nurses who had come to help the flood victims gave up and went home. The problem was too large, they said, for their aid to make any difference. Steinbeck disagreed. He wrote to Elizabeth Otis

Migrant pea pickers camp in the rain.

I.

To the red country and part of the grey country of Oklahoma, the last rains came gently and they did not cut the scarred earth. The plows crossed and recrossed the rivulet marks. The last rains lifted the corn quickly and scattered weed colonies and grass along the sides of the roads so that the grey country and the dark red country began to disappear under a green cover. In the last part of May the sky grew pale and the clouds that had hung in high puffs for so long in the spring were dissipated. The sun flared down on the growing corn day after day until a line of brown spread along the edge of each green bayonet. The clouds appeared and went away and in a while they did not try any more. The weeds grew darker green to protect themselves and they did not spread any more. The surface of the earth crusted, a thin hard crust, and as the sky became pale so the earth became pale, pink in the red country and white in the grey country. In the water cut gulleys, the earth dusted down in dry little streams. Gophers and ant lions started small avalanches. And as the sharp sun struck day after day the leaves of the young corn became less stiff and erect; they bent in a curve at first and then as the central ribs of strength grew weak, each leaf tilted downward. Then it was June and the sun shone more fiercely. The brown lines on the corn leaves, widened and moved in on the central ribs. The weeds frayed and moved back toward their roots. The air was thin and the sky more pale and every day the earth paled. In the roads where the teams moved, where the wheels milled the ground and the hooves of the horses beat the ground, the dirt crust broke and the dust formed. Every moving thing lifted the dust into the air; a walking man lifted a cloud as high as his waist, and a wagon lifted the dust as high as the fence tops, and an automobile boiled a cloud behind it. The dust was long in settling back again. When June was half gone, the big clouds moved up out of Texas and the gulf, high, heavy clouds, rain-heads. The men in the fields looked up at the clouds and sniffed at them and held wet fingers up to sense the wind. And the horses were nervous while the clouds were up. The rain heads dropped a little spattering rain and hurried on to some other country. Behind them the sky was pale again and the sun flared. In the dust there were drop craters where the rain had fallen, and there were clean splashes on the corn and that was all. A gentle wind followed the rain clouds driving them on northward, a wind that clashed the drying corn softly. A day went by and the wind increased, steady unbroken by gusts. The dust from the roads fluffed up and spread out and fell on the weeds beside the fields and fell into the fields a little way. Now the wind grew strong and hard, and worked at the rain crust in the corn fields. Little by little the sky was darkened by the mixing dust, and the wind felt over the earth, loosened the dust and carried it away. The wind was stronger. The rain crust broke and the dust lifted up out of the fields and drove grey plumes into the air like sluggish smoke. The corn threshed the air and made a dry rushing sound. The finest dust did not settle back to earth now but disappeared into the darkening sky. The wind grew stronger, whisked under stones, carried up straws and old leaves, and even little clods

The first page of the ledger in which Steinbeck wrote The Grapes of Wrath.

that "the argument that one person's effort can't really do anything doesn't seem to apply when you come on a bunch of starving children and you have a little money."

At last, home again and dry, John Steinbeck felt ready to write his book and to do it well. He opened a ledger and wrote, "To the red country and part of the gray country of Oklahoma, the last rains came gently, and they did not cut the scarred earth." He described how the rain stopped falling and the crops dried up and died. He wrote about the women and men who tied handkerchiefs over their faces to protect against the dust.

He started writing in May 1938 and stuck to a strict schedule, striving to put down two thousand words a day, five days a week. He warmed up each day by writing letters or making entries in a diary. Those activities, he said, helped "to loosen up a creaking mind."

Steinbeck found that listening to music enabled him to create pleasing rhythms in his sentences. He especially liked hearing the ballet *Swan Lake*, by Tchaikovsky, and the *Symphony of Psalms*, by Stravinsky. Sometimes, though, he had to be satisfied with the noisy chugging of the washing machine.

It was impossible to work without interruption. Carol went to the hospital in July to have her tonsils out. John made no progress while she was away. Pascal Covici's firm was in financial trouble, and this caused worry.

The sound of hammering came through the windows. Houses were going up around the Steinbeck home, which meant that John and Carol would lose their privacy. They bought an old ranch several miles away and contracted to have a house built on the property. John often had to stop writing to check on the construction.

World events occupied his mind as well. Adolf Hitler, the leader of Germany's Nazi government, had begun a campaign to dominate Europe. Germany annexed neighboring Austria in March 1938. In September, the Germans overran part of Czechoslovakia, threatening war with any country that tried to stop them.

"Everything in the world is happening and I must sit here and write," Steinbeck jotted in his diary.

In spite of the distractions, he filled the pages of his ledger, and Carol typed what he had written. It was an exhausting task. John put so much of himself into his work that he confided to his diary, "When this book is finished a goodly part of my life will be finished with it."

He felt driven to make this book the best one he had ever written. "My life isn't very long and I must get *one* good book written before it ends," he stated.

The Steinbecks finished the book—more than 200,000 words—in December 1938. The work had been so grueling that Carol fell ill again. John developed a painful infection in his leg that would take a year to heal.

John Steinbeck wanted the new novel to be "a truly American book," with a truly American title. Carol found the perfect title in the lyrics of "The Battle Hymn of the Republic," the famous Civil War song by Julia Ward Howe. Carol proposed calling the book *The Grapes of Wrath*.

Ripened grapes spill their flavorful juice when they are pressed for wine. The migrant families were ripe with wrath, or anger, that was ready to spill forth. Steinbeck wrote, "In the souls of the people the grapes of wrath are filling and growing heavy, growing heavy for the vintage."

In *The Grapes of Wrath*, Steinbeck created a family of Oklahoma farmers. He followed this family, the Joads, on their trek to California. A large extended family begins the trip. It includes Ma and Pa Joad and their grown sons, Tom, Noah, and Al. A married daughter, Rose of Sharon, and her husband come along, as well as the Joads' younger children, two grandparents, and an uncle.

The Joads allow Jim Casy, a former preacher, to travel with them. Casy has stopped preaching because he has changed his beliefs. He has come to view the world in a nonteleological way. "There ain't no sin and there ain't no virtue. There's just stuff people do," Casy explains.

The Joads prepare to leave Oklahoma in the film version of The Grapes of Wrath.

He believes that, somehow, all human beings are part of something larger. "Maybe all men got one big soul ever'body's a part of," he says.

As they drive west, the Joads see their family splinter. The grandparents die. Noah and Rose of Sharon's husband, Connie, go off on their own. More and more, the remaining family members need the support and friendship of other migrants. The Joads ration their dwindling food supply, and they share with others even worse off than they are.

Twenty families might camp beside a road together, Steinbeck writes. "In the evening a strange thing happened: the twenty families became one family, the children were the children of all." The families form a phalanx, a large body of people moving west.

At last, the Joads reach California. Steinbeck writes about the abundance they see in his home state's farm country. He describes valleys that resemble seas of blossoming fruit trees and rows of grapevines that show the promise of new growth. Such scenes contrast sharply with the hunger and poverty of the migrants.

The former preacher, Jim Casy, finds a place for himself as a union organizer. He is quickly killed in a clash with thugs hired by the growers. Hotheaded Tom Joad murders a vigilante in that fight. Pursued by the authorities, he, too, dedicates himself to working for the migrants' welfare. Tom recalls Casy's teachings about one large human soul. In a well-known passage from the book, he explains that no matter where he goes, he will always be with his people in spirit:

> Wherever they's a fight so hungry people can eat, I'll be there. . . . why, I'll be in the way guys yell when they're mad an'—I'll be in the way kids laugh when they're hungry an' they know supper's ready. An' when our folks eat the stuff they raise an' live in the houses they build—why, I'll be there.

The Joads experience many aspects of migrant life that Steinbeck witnessed firsthand. They scramble for jobs picking peaches at low wages. They are harassed by wary Californians. They even spend some time at Weedpatch.

The author drew on Tom Collins's reports to make the scenes in camp realistic. At one point in the novel, Ma Joad talks with other Weedpatch residents about ways to save toilet paper. A woman tells her, "One lady says we oughta have a little bell that rings ever' time the roll turns oncet."

The Joads leave Weedpatch to find work. But winter arrives, and with it rain. The family is driven to seek shelter from flooding in an empty railroad boxcar. There, Rose of Sharon, who is pregnant and malnourished, gives birth to a child who never breathes.

The floodwater rises above the boxcar floor. The Joads flee to higher ground and enter a barn. They are not alone. A boy is there, sitting beside an aging man who is starving and barely alive. In the final scene of the novel, Rose of Sharon understands what she must do. Her breasts are heavy with milk for the child who did not live. She feeds the starving man from her breast.

At last, Steinbeck used the story he had heard so long ago from the young drifter, Frank Kilkenny.

Rose of Sharon's kindness to a stranger does nothing to solve the huge problems that her family and the other migrants face. However, through her small act, Steinbeck shows that people can best survive by caring for one another.

Steinbeck had experimented again while writing *The Grapes of Wrath*. The book's even-numbered chapters tell the story of the Joads. The odd-numbered chapters deal with general subjects, from the way used-car salesmen took advantage of desperate people to how the migrants amused themselves in their roadside camps.

In one of the most famous odd-numbered chapters, Steinbeck describes a turtle crossing an Oklahoma highway. The turtle's journey is a metaphor for the migration of the uprooted farmers. Like the Joads and the other migrants, the turtle moves steadily on its course. It overcomes obstacles—the highway embankment that seems like a hill, and the concrete shoulder of the road, which is a tough wall to climb.

A truck driver tries to thwart the turtle's progress. As soon as the driver sees the turtle on the road, he swerves to hit it. "His front wheel struck the edge of the shell, flipped the turtle like a tiddly-wink, spun it like a coin, and rolled it off the highway," Steinbeck writes. Stuck on its back, the turtle is delayed but not defeated. The turtle, like the migrants, will keep moving forward. "The old humorous eyes looked ahead," Steinbeck writes, "and the horny beak opened a little."

As he finished his book, Steinbeck thought about the two people who had made it possible: his wife, Carol, and the hardworking camp manager, Tom Collins. He dedicated *The Grapes of Wrath*, "To CAROL who willed it. To TOM who lived it."

CHAPTER 7

A Poem, a Stink, a Grating Noise

Steinbeck's new book was published in 1939, and it caused an uproar. Most Americans had grown used to the sight of hungry people lined up outside soup kitchens, and of men selling apples on street corners. Such scenes were common in the 1930s. *The Grapes of Wrath* brought a new and troubling depression image to the public's attention: the homeless Oklahoma family wandering California's highways.

Little had been reported about the poor conditions in which the uprooted farm families lived. Readers could hardly believe that the desperation Steinbeck described was real.

The Associated Farmers, determined to protect their image and their cheap labor source, launched a campaign to defame Steinbeck and discredit his work. The growers started a rumor that the migrants hated Steinbeck for portraying them in a negative way. The author was called a liar and a communist. Some hate groups, mimicking the tactics of Nazi Germany, denounced Steinbeck as a Jew.

Such appeals to people's prejudice discouraged John Steinbeck. "I am sad for a time when one must know a man's race before his work can be approved or disapproved," he commented in a letter to one of his critics. "It happens that I am not Jewish and have no Jewish blood but it only happens that way. I find that I do not experience any pride that it is so."

Eleanor Roosevelt, wife of President Franklin Roosevelt, visited the migrant camps in California. Mrs. Roosevelt cared deeply about the welfare of people everywhere. Americans knew she would not hesitate to speak the truth. Mrs. Roosevelt confirmed that the scenes Steinbeck depicted were accurate. "I have never believed that *The Grapes of Wrath* was exaggerated," she told a reporter.

Steinbeck sent the First Lady a grateful letter. "I have been called a liar so constantly that sometimes I wonder whether I may not have dreamed the things I saw and heard in the period of my research," he wrote.

The publicity prompted Wisconsin Senator Robert M. La Follette, Jr., to investigate the use of violence against farm workers in California. La Follette and other senators heard testimony from laborers, growers, and police. They concluded that the workers' civil rights "are repeatedly and flagrantly violated." The Senate committee called for legislation to protect the migrant workers' rights.

The Grapes of Wrath created a stir for another reason as well. Its ending—a young woman nursing a grown man at her breast—shocked many readers. They accused Steinbeck of using obscenity to sell books. Officials in Buffalo, New York; East St. Louis, Illinois; and Kern County, California, banned the novel.

There were several critics who complained that the ending was unsatisfying. Steinbeck had failed to resolve the Joads' dilemma, they said. The novelist replied that those critics missed the point of his book. As he explained to Pascal Covici, he had tried "to rip a reader's nerves to rags, I don't want him satisfied."

Like the striking apple pickers of *In Dubious Battle*, the southwestern migrants were trapped in a situation for which no happy ending seemed in sight. Steinbeck had wanted to capture reality in his writing. "I tried to write this book the way lives are being lived not the way books are written," he stated.

Many critics, however, praised *The Grapes of Wrath*. A writer for the *North American Review*, a literary journal, called the novel "momentous, monumental, and memorable." Steinbeck had created "the highest art," the critic wrote.

Others thought it was an important book, but not one of the best written in recent years. An article in *The New Republic* stated that "it doesn't rank with the best of Hemingway or Dos Passos. But it belongs very high in the category of the great angry books like 'Uncle Tom's Cabin' that have roused a people to fight against intolerable wrongs."

Some reviewers griped about Steinbeck's "sentimentalism," his emphasis on emotion over reason. Critics would often complain about the strong emotional quality of Steinbeck's work in the years ahead. They would claim that it weakened his books. Yet, curiously, the feelings he communicated helped to make Steinbeck a favorite of many readers.

Twentieth Century Fox, a motion picture company, soon began filming *The Grapes of Wrath*. At Steinbeck's suggestion, the producers hired Tom Collins as a technical advisor. Collins made sure the film portrayed migrant life accurately. He arranged for some scenes to be filmed at Weedpatch.

The folk singer Woody Guthrie told the story of *The Grapes of Wrath* in a song titled "Tom Joad." Guthrie wrote the song, he said, "because the people back in Oklahoma haven't got two bucks to buy the book, or even thirty-five cents to see the movie, but the song will get back to them and tell them what Preacher Casy said."

In 1940, Steinbeck won the Pulitzer Prize for fiction for *The Grapes of Wrath*. Columbia University presents the Pulitzer Prizes every year for outstanding achievements in journalism and literature. Steinbeck gave the prize money—one thousand dollars—to an aspiring writer, Ritch Lovejoy, to further his career. The novel also earned Steinbeck an appointment to the National Institute of Arts and Letters, an elite society of writers, artists, and composers.

The Steinbecks now had famous friends. The silent film star Charlie Chaplin was a frequent visitor at their ranch. The actor Burgess Meredith, who played George Milton in the film *Of Mice and Men*, became one of John's close friends.

John also befriended Pare Lorentz, a well-known documentary film-maker. Lorentz was making a series of films on America in the depression for the federal government. John worked with him on *The Fight for Life*, a film showing the hazards of childbirth for the poor.

But fame had a downside. Suddenly, everyone wanted something from John Steinbeck. Civic groups invited him to make speeches, and strangers asked him for money. Letters arrived at the Steinbeck home—thirty, forty, or more each day. The telephone rang constantly. John hated to speak on the phone, calling it "a thing of horror." So Carol took most of the calls. The attention was distressing. "Why do they think a writer, just because he can write, will make a good after-dinner speaker, or a club committee man—or even a public leader?" John asked a reporter for the *Los Angeles Times*.

Steinbeck wanted to get away from the phone and the mail. He wanted to stop being a famous author and go back to being what he had been: an unknown writer working undisturbed. He decided to turn away from fiction and write about science. Surely, no one would try to make a science writer into a celebrity!

He and Ed Ricketts came up with a plan to write books about the animals of the western coastal waters. They would start in the Gulf of California, the long narrow body of water that separates Baja California from the mainland of Mexico. The gulf once had been called the Sea of Cortez, after the Spaniard who explored the region in the sixteenth century.

John, Ed, and Carol chartered a boat, the *Western Flyer*. They stocked it with provisions and hired a crew. On March 11, 1940, they set sail from Monterey and headed south.

They stopped in San Diego, California, for food and fuel. San Diego, close to the Mexican border, is the site of a large naval base. John and the others saw stockpiles of bombs and torpedoes on the military base. Planes flew overhead in formation, and ships and submarines sat idle

John and Carol Steinbeck, second and third from right, pose with friends and crewmen aboard the Western Flyer. *(Courtesy of the Steinbeck Research Center, San Jose State University)*

Navy destroyers in the waters off San Diego prior to World War II.

in the water. "All about us war bustled, although we had no war," Steinbeck wrote in the book that chronicled the journey, *The Sea of Cortez*.

Europe, however, did have a war. On September 1, 1939, the German army had marched into Poland. When England and France responded by declaring war on Germany, World War II began. Now the Soviet Union, headed by the dictator Joseph Stalin, was threatening war with its Scandinavian neighbors. Trouble was brewing in Asia, too. Japanese forces had occupied sections of China. Many Americans feared that the United States would soon be drawn into these conflicts.

John Steinbeck felt glad to be traveling away from news of the world's problems. "There are things in the tide pools easier to understand than Stalinist, Hitlerite, Democrat, capitalist confusion, and voodoo," he wrote to Dook Sheffield.

Along the Mexican shoreline, John, Ed, and the crew collected worms and crabs, sponges and sea cucumbers. It was a challenge to catch the swift, agile crabs known as Sally Lightfoots. "They appear to read the mind of their hunter," Steinbeck observed. No matter what method the captors tried, the Sally Lightfoots stayed out of reach. It took a long time to gather a few specimens, although many of the red, blue, and brown crabs scurried over the rocks.

John gathered stories in Mexico as well. In the city of La Paz, he heard about a young Indian who found an oyster containing a very large pearl. The pearl was valuable enough to make him wealthy for the rest of his life. Soon, tricksters tried to make the boy sell the pearl for a small sum. Thieves beat him while he slept and searched his clothing for the jewel. The boy saw that his wealth brought out the worst in other people. He cursed the pearl and threw it back into the sea.

That story took root and thrived in Steinbeck's imagination. It would be the inspiration for his short novel *The Pearl*, published in 1947.

The *Western Flyer* returned to its dock in Monterey on April 20. Soon, John was back in Mexico making a film, *The Forgotten Village*. It dealt

A German news photograph shows a Nazi tank patrolling a Polish street.

with the problems public health workers faced when they tried to change the habits of uneducated people. John had seen how Mexican peasants and southwestern migrants resisted advice from nurses and doctors if it contradicted their superstitions. He hoped his film would improve health care in poor communities. In spite of his resolution to stick to science, he had trouble ignoring people in need.

As he hired actors and chose locations for filming, Steinbeck was surprised to see Nazi propaganda being circulated in Mexico. He wrote a letter to President Roosevelt about what he had seen, and he later met with the president in Washington, D.C. He offered to help the government in any way possible.

John was constantly busy, but none of his activity could cover up a painful fact. He and Carol were growing apart. They had gotten along well when they were poor and struggling. Now, John's success strained their relationship. They separated in April 1941.

Lonely and upset, John visited Ed Ricketts in his lab. He recalled in "About Ed Ricketts" how his friend played music for him that was "like medicine. Late in the night when he should have been asleep, he played music for me on his great phonograph—even when I was asleep he played it, knowing that its soothing would get into my dark confusion."

John's emotions improved as the weeks passed. He and Ed finished their book, *The Sea of Cortez*. But seeing old friends and familiar places reminded John of happier times with Carol. He wanted to make a fresh start, so he moved to New York City again.

Before he had time to settle in an apartment, though, he was called to Washington, D.C. The government was forming an agency to combat propaganda from the Axis nations—Germany, Japan, and their ally, Italy. Agency officials had learned of Steinbeck's conversation with the president and they asked him to help.

It was October 1941. Within weeks, the United States was at war. On December 7, Japanese fighter planes and submarines attacked the U.S. naval base at Pearl Harbor, Hawaii. Congress responded by declaring war on Japan. Days later, Germany and Italy announced that they, too, were at war with the United States. American troops were soon fighting battles in the South Pacific, Europe, and North Africa.

Americans felt united in their effort to win the war. Young men enlisted in the armed forces by the thousands. The war ended the plight of the Dust Bowl migrants. Many of them joined the service or went to work in factories building warships and airplanes.

John Steinbeck poured his energy into his government work. And he returned to writing fiction. He completed a novel, *The Moon Is Down*, that was set in an unnamed European country. Published in 1942, it showed what life might be like under the control of an occupying army like the Nazis.

Once more, Steinbeck's writing stirred up conflicting opinions. Critics argued that *The Moon Is Down* made the conquering army appear too human. Instead of looking for the good in the soldiers, they said, Steinbeck should have portrayed them as evil beings. His viewpoint was much too romantic.

Some worried that the novel would hamper America's war effort. The author James Thurber warned that "we might yet lose the war. Nothing would help more toward that end than for Americans to believe the Steinbeck version of Nazi conquest."

People living in the occupied countries of Europe, however, admired *The Moon Is Down*. They said it portrayed their situation accurately. They read the book in secret, passing worn, smuggled-in copies to their friends. Germany had made it a crime to possess Steinbeck's novel.

In the 1960s, Steinbeck received a tattered, mimeographed copy of *The Moon Is Down* in the mail. A Danish fan who had valued the book during wartime now wanted the author to have it. Knocking his earlier critics, Steinbeck said of his novel, "the closer it got to action, the less romantic it seemed."

John and Carol Steinbeck were divorced in March 1943. John married again quickly. His new wife was Gwyn Conger, a dancer and actress.

Just months after the wedding, John sailed for Europe. He had been hired by the *Herald Tribune*, a New York newspaper, to report on the war.

While the other war correspondents wrote about battles and military tactics, Steinbeck covered the human side of the war. For example, he visited an air base in Britain and described flight crews dressing for bombing missions. "During the process the men have gotten bigger and bigger as layer on layer of equipment is put on. They walk stiffly, like artificial men," he noted.

He told how the men placed treasured objects under their pillows before leaving on a mission. That way, if they were shot down, others could send their jewelry, letters, and photographs home to loved ones.

The crew of one bomber had adopted a small dog. The dog always heard the planes returning from a mission before the ground crew did. As soon as a certain plane touched down, Steinbeck wrote, "there is a sharp, crying bark and a streak of gray. The little dog seems hardly to touch the ground. He streaks across the field toward the landed ship. He knows his own ship."

In August, Steinbeck traveled to North Africa, where Americans and their allies were preparing to invade Italy. He went along with some of the American forces when they landed at Salerno, in southern Italy.

The soldiers knew that German units would be waiting to fire on them. Steinbeck wondered whether he would panic under gunfire, or whether he would maintain his courage and his cool. "No man there knows whether he can take it, knows whether he will run away or stick, or lose his nerve and go to pieces, or will be a good soldier," he wrote.

Steinbeck found that he could take it, although the sight of war upset him greatly. He wrote about the horror he witnessed at Salerno for the *Herald Tribune*. He described the sights a typical war correspondent might have seen following a battle but not reported:

> He might have seen the splash of dirt and dust that is a shell
> burst, and a small Italian girl in the street with her stomach

U.S. Coast Guard and Navy personnel hug the beach at Paesternum, near Salerno,
Italy, during a Nazi bomber attack. Debris from an exploded bomb rises in the
background.

blown out, and he might have seen an American soldier standing over a twitching body, crying. . . .

The burning odor of dust will be in his nose and the stench of men and animals killed yesterday and the day before. . . . He will smell his own sweat and the accumulated sweat of an army. When his throat is dry he will drink the warm water from his canteen, which tastes of disinfectant.

Seeing war made Steinbeck feel jittery and depressed. He returned to New York in October 1943, and those feelings persisted. Writing a novel had eased his reaction to the migrant camps, but the war was too terrible for Steinbeck to use in his fiction. Instead, he set to work on "a funny little book that is fun"—a short novel inspired by Ed Ricketts and his neighbors called *Cannery Row*.

In this book, which was published in 1945, Steinbeck used a string of metaphors to describe the eccentric community on the Monterey waterfront. "Cannery Row in Monterey in California is a poem, a stink, a grating noise, a quality of light, a tone, a habit, a nostalgia, a dream," he wrote. He summed up Cannery Row as "the gathered and scattered, tin and iron and rust and splintered wood, chipped pavement and weedy lots and junk heaps. . . ."

Capturing the neighborhood in words was a challenge for the author. He wondered how to transfer the odors, the noises, and the atmosphere of Cannery Row to the pages of a book and keep them intact.

Steinbeck felt like a biologist picking up delicate specimens at the shore. "When you collect marine animals there are certain flat worms so delicate that they are almost impossible to capture whole, for they break and tatter under the touch. You must let them ooze and crawl of their own will onto a knife blade and then lift them gently into your bottle of sea water," he explained. He chose a similar method for writing his book, "to open the page and let the stories crawl in by themselves."

Steinbeck based his characters on the offbeat people he met on

Steinbeck modeled the Palace Flophouse, home to Mack and the boys, after this building on Cannery Row. (Courtesy of the Steinbeck Research Center, San Jose State University)

Cannery Row. The characters who crawl into his novel include Mack and the boys, a group of carefree hoboes. According to the author, these men are wise to forego the rat race of modern life. "In a time when people tear themselves to pieces with ambition and nervousness and covetousness, they are relaxed," he stated. "All of our so-called successful men are sick men, with bad stomachs, and bad souls, but Mack and the boys are healthy and curiously clean."

In the character of Doc, a biologist living on Cannery Row, Steinbeck painted an affectionate portrait of Ed Ricketts. "Doc is rather small, deceptively small, for he is wiry and very strong and when passionate anger comes on him he can be very fierce. He wears a beard and his face is half Christ and half satyr and his face tells the truth," Steinbeck observed. "Doc has the hands of a brain surgeon, and a cool warm mind. Doc tips his hat to dogs as he drives by and the dogs look up and smile at him."

The Steinbecks lived in one-half of this duplex on East Seventy-eighth Street in New York City. (Courtesy of the Steinbeck Research Center, San Jose State University)

The novel describes typical happenings on Cannery Row. Mack and the boys continually try to outsmart Lee Chong, the grocer. Parties are planned and quickly get out of control. Doc patiently labors in his lab and on the shore.

To Steinbeck, Cannery Row was an ecosystem, an interdependent group of living things. Like the great tide pool at the end of the Monterey Peninsula, Cannery Row was a little world. In the tide pool and on Cannery Row, "The smells of life and richness, of death and digestion, of decay and birth, burden the air."

While he was writing *Cannery Row*, Steinbeck also busied himself with family life. He planted a garden on the small patch of land behind his house. He cooked chili for guests. He got to know the local merchants—the butcher and the news dealer. Before long, he felt at home in the city. "I was no longer a stranger," he realized. "I had become a New Yorker."

On August 2, 1944, Gwyn gave birth to a boy. The Steinbecks named him Thom. John announced to friends that Thom was "a baby-shaped baby," with red hair and blue eyes.

John, Gwyn, and baby Thom. (Courtesy of the Steinbeck Research Center, San Jose State University)

A year later, World War II came to an end. On May 8, 1945, the United States and Great Britain declared victory in Europe. Japan surrendered in August, after the United States destroyed the cities of Hiroshima and Nagasaki with atomic bombs. With the depression now a painful memory, Americans looked forward to raising families in peace and prosperity. The Steinbecks had a second child in June 1946. He was a boy named John, whom his father nicknamed Catbird. Steinbeck started work on a "big book," one that delved into the history of the Salinas Valley.

Then on May 7, 1948, John learned some terrible news. Ed Ricketts had been driving in his car when it was hit by a train. Ed was alive, but very badly hurt. He was in a hospital and scheduled for surgery, but the doctors offered little hope.

John could not hold back his tears. "The greatest man in the world is dying and there is nothing I can do," he cried. He flew to California, but by the time he arrived, Ed Ricketts was dead.

The funeral took place in a chapel overlooking the Pacific Ocean. John took one look at the coffin and flowers and decided this was not the way to say good-bye to his friend. He walked down to the beach, where he sat on a rock and watched the water flow in the tide pools. One by one, other mourners followed him. Soon, a small group of friends bade farewell to Ed on the shore that he loved.

Wearily, John flew back to New York. As soon as he got home, he was in for another shock. Gwyn told him that she no longer loved him. She wanted a divorce.

CHAPTER 8

Joy

With Ed dead and his family breaking up, John Steinbeck felt the deepest despair he had ever known. He returned to his old house in Pacific Grove to live, but made several trips to Mexico. He said he was writing the script for a film on the life of Emiliano Zapata, a Mexican revolutionary leader. He accomplished very little, though. Mostly he roamed the streets of Mexican towns, feeling like a "mad dog."

Mildred Lyman, of the McIntosh and Otis Agency, called on Steinbeck in Pacific Grove during this troubled time. She wrote a worried letter to her colleagues. "He eats at odd hours and not properly, stays up late and sleeps late and tries so hard to convince himself that he likes it," Lyman reported. "I presume he will come out of it but my only hope is that it will not be too late as far as his work is concerned."

At least Steinbeck could look forward to summertime visits from his sons. Those visits were happy times, when Thom and Catbird slept in a tent their father bought for them. John took his sons fishing. But the end of summer came quickly, bringing painful questions from the boys. "When are you coming home to New York?" they asked. "Why can't we stay here?" Their father answered sadly, "I don't know."

Steinbeck took comfort in a lesson Ed Ricketts had taught him. He recalled Ed's words in a letter to the writer Ritch Lovejoy and his wife. "This species has experienced channels for all pain and all sorrow and all happiness possible. They are ready when they are needed," Ricketts had said. In other words, over countless generations, the human species had developed ways to work through intense feelings. Steinbeck understood that his grief would subside naturally, given time.

Indeed, he soon met someone who brought love and happiness into his life. Elaine Scott had worked as a stage manager in the New York theater world. She was a friendly, down-to-earth person. John began to spend a great deal of time with Elaine, and his sorrow eased. At last, he felt ready to work again. He finished the screenplay for *Viva Zapata!*. The film was released in 1950 and was very well received.

John and Elaine were married on December 20, 1950. This marriage proved to be a lasting and happy one. The couple made their home in New York City, where John could be close to his sons. He contentedly

John and Elaine Steinbeck in the 1950s. (Courtesy of the Steinbeck Research Center, San Jose State University)

John and his sons on Nantucket.

made repairs to the home he shared with Elaine and her daughter from an earlier marriage, Waverly Scott.

In the summer of 1951, the family vacationed on Nantucket, a Massachusetts island. John fished and sailed with the children, and he felt his old silliness return. He secretly purchased a small cannon. On August 14, Elaine's birthday, he honored his new wife by firing the cannon forty-one times over the water. Members of the Coast Guard heard the racket. They motored over in a boat to find out what in the world was going on. John put on his most serious face and politely explained what he was doing. The Coast Guard gave him permission to continue.

John was now at work on the "big book" he had been thinking about before Ed's death, the book about the Salinas Valley. He wrote the book as a gift to his sons, to teach them their heritage. "They are little boys now and they will never know what they came from through me, unless I tell them," he explained.

While preparing to write this book, Steinbeck put in many hours of research. He visited the scenes of his childhood, talked to old friends and neighbors, and read back issues of a local newspaper, the *Salinas Californian*. "Newspapers accurately recorded the lives of the people in the valley," he told one of the paper's reporters. The newspaper's editorials showed Steinbeck how the people of the valley thought in years gone by.

The reporter remarked on Steinbeck's strength and "beartrap" mind. "He shakes hands like an Italian fisherman off a Monterey purse seiner —a full, strong grasp that makes another man like and respect him," the newspaperman stated. Steinbeck was "alert, intelligent, intellectual and cunning," the reporter said. "He recalls every phase of his work and can recount exact lines, phrases and words as they appear, indicating the effort that has gone into his writing."

In creating a book for his sons, two brothers, Steinbeck drew on one of the best-known stories of two brothers. The saga of the Trask family in Steinbeck's book echoes the story of Cain and Abel in the Bible.

According to the Bible, Cain and Abel were the sons of Adam and Eve. They grew to be men and began their life's work. Cain farmed the earth, while Abel tended sheep. The brothers prospered, and each brother presented an offering to God. Abel brought one of his finest animals, a gift that pleased the Lord. Cain gave from the bounty of the soil, yet his gift failed to earn God's gratitude.

Angry, perplexed, and jealous, Cain murdered his brother. As punishment for his crime, he was no longer allowed to see God's face. "And Cain went out from the presence of the Lord," the Bible states, "and dwelt in the east of Eden."

Steinbeck thought this story had importance for all people. He wrote in his new book, "I think everyone in the world to a large or small extent has felt rejection. And with rejection comes anger, and with anger some kind of crime in revenge for the rejection, and with the crime guilt—and there is the story of mankind."

Steinbeck called his big book *East of Eden*. The book follows the character Adam Trask from his childhood in Connecticut in the 1800s to his adult life in the Salinas Valley at the time of World War I.

Growing up, Adam and his brother, Charles, compete for their father's love. Charles saves his money and buys their father a fine pocketknife for his birthday. He receives only a cold "thanks" for his effort. Adam gives their father a stray puppy that costs him nothing. Adam's gift pleases their father immensely.

"That dog sleeps in his room. He plays with it while he's reading," Charles gripes. "And where's the knife? 'Thanks,' he said, just 'Thanks.' " Charles is sure his father prefers the pup because he loves Adam more. Charles is hurt, and he lashes out at his brother, giving him a severe beating.

Years later, in California, Adam Trask is the father of twin teenage sons, Cal and Aron. Adam Trask is now a broken man. He has lost his land and his money. His wife, who left him after the boys were born, works as a prostitute in Salinas. Adam has kept that fact hidden from his sons.

While Aron studies at college, Cal is determined to earn back his father's fortune. Working with a local businessman, Cal buys up crops of beans at a low price and then sells them to the government for a high profit. The government needs beans to feed to the soldiers of World War I.

Cal earns $15,000, which he presents to his father at Thanksgiving. Instead of rejoicing, however, Adam Trask rejects the gift. He tells Cal, "I would have been so happy if you could have given me—well, what your brother has—pride in the thing he's doing, gladness in his progress. Money, even clean money, doesn't stack up to that."

A deeply distressed Cal takes his feelings out on his brother. Cal has discovered the truth about their mother, and now he reveals what he knows to Aron. Upset by the news, Aron enlists in the army on impulse. He dies fighting the Germans in World War I.

The twins' mother, Cathy (who, as a prostitute, calls herself Kate), is the one character in all of Steinbeck's fiction who lacks a basic goodness. The author has trouble explaining this ruthless woman who deserts her children and destroys people's lives. He decides she is a "monster." He asks, "Can there not be mental or psychic monsters born?" Cathy was born without normal human feelings, he says. He describes her as a demon, with a pointed tongue, feet like tiny hoofs, and an evil look in her eye.

East of Eden contains the story of another family, the Hamiltons. These are real people—Steinbeck's grandparents, Samuel and Liza, and their many children, including Olive Hamilton Steinbeck. The novel relates family stories that were passed from one generation to the next. For example, it tells how Samuel Hamilton had a mind filled with plans, how he invented many gadgets but never made any money from them. The book tells how Samuel's son Tom fastened a sofa to a horse-drawn cart to drive some girls to a dance.

In *East of Eden*, Steinbeck recalls Olive's ride in an airplane during the years of World War I. At that time, wooden biplanes with open cockpits had only recently been developed. John remembers watching the plane take off and fly as far as the Spreckels Sugar Company. On the way back, the pilot performs barrel rolls and other tricks. Olive is terrified, but she keeps smiling at the pilot. He misunderstands her smile, thinks she is fearless, and so performs more treacherous stunts.

At last, the plane lands. "It took four men and quite a long time to get Olive out of the cockpit," Steinbeck writes. "She was so rigid they could not bend her. We took her home and put her to bed, and she didn't get up for two days."

Steinbeck started writing *East of Eden* in a large bound notebook. He wrote the novel on the right-hand pages only. On the left-hand pages, he composed letters to his editor, Pascal Covici. Writing these letters each morning helped him warm up for the day's work. The letters are a record of the author's thinking as he developed his novel. They were published in 1969 as a separate book, *Journal of a Novel.*

In his letters to Covici, Steinbeck expressed his frustration when the work progressed slowly. He wrote, "The human mind I believe is nothing but a muscle. Sometimes it has tone and sometimes not. And mine is not in very good tone right now. It is jumbled and slow and like a bad child." Steinbeck also communicated his happiness when the work went well. "This is a time of great joy," he wrote one day. "It will never be so good again—never. A book finished, published, read—is always anticlimax to me. The joy comes in the words going down and the rhythms crowding in the chest and pulsing to get out."

Steinbeck's letters to Pascal Covici reveal the small details of a writer's life as well. "On the third finger of my right hand I have a great callus just from using a pencil for so many hours every day," he wrote. "It has become a big lump by now and it doesn't ever go away. Sometimes it is very rough and other times, as today, it is as shiny as glass."

Creating his long, complicated saga of two families was a very difficult task. Steinbeck sometimes doubted that he had enough talent to succeed. Still, he set a high standard for himself and did his best to reach it. "A good writer always works at the impossible," he believed.

East of Eden was published in 1952, and it was another best-seller for John Steinbeck. The author had produced "a strange and original work of art," one critic said. Another proclaimed, "This is certainly his best book since 'The Grapes of Wrath' and, I believe, evidence that he has been thinking more deeply than ever about life and the human beings who live it."

With his book finished, Steinbeck was ready for a change of scenery. He and Elaine left on a long trip to Europe in March 1952. It was the first of many overseas journeys for the couple.

John was an energetic tourist. He visited art museums and studied the architecture of Spain. He walked all over Paris to view the Arc de Triomphe, the Eiffel Tower, and other famous sights. Fascinated by tools and gizmos, he browsed in every foreign hardware store that he spotted. He wrote about his travels for *Collier's* magazine.

John and Elaine visited Louis Gibey, a teacher living in the Jura Mountains, between France and Switzerland. Gibey had written letters to Steinbeck, who was one of his favorite authors. In Gibey's village, the Steinbecks tasted local wines. They discussed politics and hunting dogs with their host and his neighbors. "People like these are the soul and guts of France," Steinbeck concluded. The men and women he met were "hardy and hard-working." The men of the region had fought bravely against Germany during World War II. Many had been wounded, and some had been taken prisoner. Still, Steinbeck wrote, "They were not broken. They remain incorrigible individuals, no two holding opinions exactly alike."

In Northern Ireland, John and Elaine located the old Hamilton house, where his grandfather had lived before settling in California. John hoped to meet some Irish relatives and to feel a bond with his heritage, but the family in Ireland had died out. None of the local people remembered Samuel Hamilton. "I went to see the house and there was nothing of us there," Steinbeck wrote. "The new owners were kind. But they were strangers, and, what was even worse, we were strangers."

The Steinbecks made another trip to Europe in 1954. In West Germany, John prepared a statement for Radio Free Europe. This organization broadcasted to the communist countries of Eastern Europe, countries that had fallen under Soviet domination after World War II. The governments of those nations controlled citizens' access to news and information. They banned many books by Western authors. Writers in those countries could not publish books or articles that criticized the government or the communist way of life.

Steinbeck welcomed this chance to address people who were forbidden to read his novels. His statement contained words of friendship. "There was a time when I could visit you and you were free to visit me," he wrote. "My books were in your stores and you were free to

John, Elaine, and the boys practice their marksmanship in Paris in 1954. Thom and Catbird spent part of the summer in Europe with their father and stepmother.

The Sag Harbor cottage.

write to me on any subject. Now your borders are closed with barbed wire and guarded by armed men and fierce dogs, not to keep me out but to keep you in. And now your minds are also imprisoned. You are told that I am a bad writer but you are not permitted to judge for yourselves."

Steinbeck urged his audience to keep their minds open. "You must remember and teach your children that they are precious," he stated, "not as dull cogs in the wheel of party existence, but as units, complete and shining in themselves."

He wanted to read the statement on the radio himself, but this meant learning to say his words in several languages. He practiced for hours until he could recite his statement in Czech, the principal language of Czechoslovakia. Foreign languages did not come easily to Steinbeck, though. He gave up on trying to learn the Polish, Rumanian, and Hungarian versions of his statement and let others read it in those languages.

During the 1954 trip, John and Elaine traveled to the French town of Blois. When they reached their hotel, John said he felt weak. He was perspiring, and his face was flushed. Suddenly, he passed out. A French doctor who examined him said that John might have had sunstroke. The Steinbecks had been riding in a convertible car with the top down. John rested in bed for several days, and he felt better. He never knew for certain what caused his illness.

The Steinbecks returned to the United States when winter was on its way. John clearly felt at home now in New York City, but he missed country life. He and Elaine bought a cottage in the village of Sag Harbor, on eastern Long Island, for summers and weekends. Sag Harbor had been a center for whaling in the nineteenth century. The old homes on Sag Harbor's main streets once had belonged to prosperous whalers. Many featured widow's walks, windowed chambers atop their roofs where residents could watch for returning ships.

The Steinbecks' small house was on a bluff beside a cove. There was a dock on the property, so John bought a boat for fishing. He seldom

Steinbeck's retreat, Joyous Garde.

caught any fish, but he had fun trying. He got to know the mayor of Sag Harbor, the police chief, the grocer, and the owner of the local hardware store. He got up early in Sag Harbor and drove in to town for breakfast and a newspaper. He often brought Elaine's standard poodle, Charley, who liked to ride in cars.

In Sag Harbor, John Steinbeck found a quiet joy. He learned to identify the plants and wildlife of eastern Long Island. The trees, bushes, and birds that he saw were different from the ones he had grown up with in California. He built a nest high up in a dead tree for a pair of ospreys, fishing birds that return to the same nesting places each spring.

He also built a workplace for himself in Sag Harbor. It was a small, hexagonal structure where he could write undisturbed. With windows on all of its sides, the building reminded Steinbeck of "a little lighthouse," he said. He could look out at the water, his house, or his garden as he wrote. Steinbeck named the shelter Joyous Garde, after a castle in the first book he had loved, *Morte d'Arthur*.

Betty Furness became a celebrity in the 1950s by displaying home appliances on television for the Westinghouse Corporation.

CHAPTER 9

John Steinbeck, Knight

Life was good for most Americans in the 1950s. Workers felt secure in their jobs. They often earned enough to support their families and to afford the goods that American industry produced. The automobile factories in Detroit, Michigan, turned out eight million cars in 1955, many more than the two million that were built in 1946. Although fewer than 17,000 families owned a television set in 1946, stores were selling more than 250,000 TVs every month within a few years.

It was a time of conformity in appearance and in thought. Society looked with suspicion on the beatniks, men and women who turned away from materialism to pursue artistic and intellectual goals. At least those rebels, with their sandals and berets, were easy to spot. But, some people worried, what if there were individuals who dressed like everyone else yet embraced dangerous—even communist—ideas?

With the Soviet Union now dominating Eastern Europe, many Americans feared the spread of communism. A communist government had seized power in China in 1949. In the early 1950s, American troops had taken part in the Korean War. That war began on June 25, 1950, when the communist North Korean army, aided and equipped by the Soviet Union, invaded South Korea. The Americans were part of a United Nations force that repelled the communist invaders.

At home, Congress engaged in a witch hunt, searching for communists in American society. In 1947, several movie screenwriters and directors were summoned to testify before the House Un-American Activities Committee about ties to communism in their past. The committee also went after scientists, educators, government workers, and writers.

Some witnesses cooperated with the congressional committee, but others were outraged and declined to testify. They risked going to prison for being in contempt of Congress, rather than go along with a process that violated their rights as citizens.

The playwright Arthur Miller was summoned to testify in the spring of 1957. Miller had come to the committee's attention for writing plays such as *Death of a Salesman* (1949), which looked critically at widely accepted values. He had even written a play about a colonial witch trial, *The Crucible* (1953), that had been inspired by the committee's activities.

As a young man, Miller had attended meetings where communist writers were present. The congressmen now asked him to name other people who had been at those meetings, but Miller refused to do so. No one at those meetings had been a traitor, and Miller would not jeopardize anyone's reputation or career. The committee found him to be in contempt of Congress.

The treatment of Arthur Miller by the United States government was a threat to all American writers. If Miller could be questioned and jailed because a few people in Congress objected to his writings, so could anyone. Yet only one author, John Steinbeck, came to Miller's defense.

In an essay published in *Esquire* magazine, Steinbeck wrote, "In Hitler's Germany, it was considered patriotic to report your friends and relations to the authorities. And we in America have felt safe from and superior to these things. But are we so safe or superior?" He continued, "If I were in Arthur Miller's shoes, I do not know what I would do. But I could wish, for myself and for my children, that I would be brave enough to fortify and defend my private morality as he has."

(Miller was later fined five hundred dollars and sentenced to a month in jail, but his sentence was suspended.)

In his willingness to fight against society's wrongs, Steinbeck was like the knights of an earlier age. He traced the knightly aspects of his character—his ideas of right and wrong, his sense of social responsibility, and his gallantry—back to his childhood reading about King Arthur.

It disappointed Steinbeck that his sons' generation, used to television and motion pictures, had no patience for reading old books like Sir Thomas Malory's *Morte d'Arthur*. The young people were missing the pleasures and lessons to be gained from this great work of literature.

Steinbeck wondered, what if someone were to tell Malory's tales in modern English? Would people want to read them? The more he kicked around this idea, the better he liked it. He decided to rewrite the great book himself.

The project captivated his imagination. For the next few years, Steinbeck bored the people around him with talk of King Arthur, Malory, and the Middle Ages. Elizabeth Otis remarked that if she heard the name Malory one more time, she would scream!

Steinbeck began the project in the simplest way, by replacing the archaic words in Malory's text with modern ones, and by shortening Malory's long, difficult sentences. But the result fell short of what he wanted to achieve.

He wished he could get inside the medieval author's mind, to know how Malory thought. He read everything he could find on Malory's life and times. He struck up a friendship with Professor Eugène Vinaver, an expert on Malory at a university in England. He even went to Europe to visit the scenes of Malory's life.

Back in Sag Harbor, though, Steinbeck's writing frustrated him. Again and again, he started to write his Arthurian tales, but every attempt was a failure. No matter how hard he tried, he could not duplicate the beauty and depth of Malory's work.

Elaine Steinbeck saw how discouraged her husband was. She suggested that they spend a long time in Somerset, the county in southern England where King Arthur is said to have lived.

The Steinbecks moved into a small Somerset cottage in February

1959. John thrived in the rustic setting. He chopped wood for the fireplace, and he planted vegetables. He studied the interiors of castles so that he could describe them accurately in his book. With Eugène Vinaver at his side, he wandered the English countryside. It looked odd to see John Steinbeck, tall, ruddy, and dressed in hiking clothes, crossing hills and meadows with the small, polished professor in his well-tailored suit.

At last, John started to write. A relieved Elaine wrote to friends in the States that he was excited about his work and at peace with himself. "The impatience, and the alternating black moods and wrought-up-ness are gone," Elaine wrote. "*That* nightmare is over, I think."

In just a few months, John completed his versions of six of the many episodes in the saga of King Arthur. As he wrote, he reflected on his childhood games of chivalry. He dedicated his book to his companion in those games, his sister Mary. "And from this hour she shall be called Sir Marie Steinbeck of Salinas Valley. God give her worship without peril," he decreed. He signed the dedication, "John Steinbeck of Monterey, Knight."

Steinbeck read over the tales he had written and found that they still disappointed him. Maybe he was trying to do the impossible—but that was no reason to quit. He wrote to Eugène Vinaver, "You see a writer—like a knight—must aim at perfection, and failing, not fall back on the cushion that there is no perfection. He must believe himself capable of perfection even when he fails."

And so, when Steinbeck turned away from his work on King Arthur, he told himself that he would come back to it one day. He had not given up. "I come toward the ending of my life with the same ache for perfection I had as a child," he wrote.

As a knight waging battles with his pen, John Steinbeck now attacked the materialism and greed of modern society. In Somerset, with few possessions to distract him, he had found contentment. How that simple life contrasted with the scramble to acquire and get ahead that he witnessed at home! So many Americans competed with their neighbors to be the first to own the latest model car or appliance. People seemed all too ready to abandon their morals for money. News reports told of quiz show contestants who were fed the answers to questions, and radio disc jockeys who took money from record companies to promote certain songs.

Steinbeck worried about the effect this social climate would have on his sons. "It is very hard to raise boys to love and respect virtue and learning when the tools of success are chicanery, treachery, self-interest, laziness and cynicism," he said in a letter to Dag Hammarskjöld, secretary-general of the United Nations. In another letter, to the statesman Adlai Stevenson, he predicted that America's wealth would be its downfall: "If I wanted to destroy a nation, I would give it too much and I would have it on its knees, miserable, greedy and sick."

That letter was printed in the Long Island newspaper *Newsday*, and it caused controversy. John Steinbeck was becoming a cranky old curmudgeon, many people said. He had failed to keep up with the times. Others, such as the poet Carl Sandburg, disagreed. "Anything John Steinbeck says about this country—about us as a nation—is worth careful reading and study," Sandburg commented. "His record of love for his country and service for it is such that what he says is important."

Steinbeck then wielded a larger weapon against the nation's eroding values. It was his last novel, *The Winter of Our Discontent*. The book tells of a man who is dissatisfied with his life. Ethan Allen Hawley descended from a wealthy family. Now, with the Hawley fortune gone, he works as a clerk in a grocery store. He cannot afford the car or television that his family wants.

Ethan questions the wisdom of being honest as he watches his town's leaders profit from shady business deals. His own teenage son sees nothing wrong with cheating, because, "everybody does it. It's the way the cooky crumbles." Ethan launches a crooked plan of his own, to take over the store where he works. His scheme involves robbing the bank and destroying the lives of two men.

A chance occurrence stops Ethan from becoming a robber, and his

A family portrait from 1961: sons John and Thom, John, and Elaine.

daughter leads him back to the values that guided him in the past. Ethan has done damage to others, though, that cannot be undone. He will have to live with the results of his actions. In the future, Ethan will struggle to be a lantern of honesty in a dark, corrupt world.

The Winter of Our Discontent is set in New Baytown, New York, a fictional village that resembles Sag Harbor. The action takes place between Good Friday and the Fourth of July, 1960, which was just when Steinbeck wrote the book. If he wanted to describe the weather in his story, the author had only to look out the window of Joyous Garde to see what it was like.

Shortly before he started writing *The Winter of Our Discontent*, Steinbeck had another mysterious attack of ill health. This time, he was smoking in his New York City home when he felt weak and lost consciousness. Elaine discovered what had happened just in time. She put out the fire that John's cigarette had started and got him to a hospital.

As John recovered again, Elaine worried. She kept watch on him as he wrote his novel. She begged him not to go out on his boat alone, and not to work too hard around the house. John complained that Elaine was acting like a "stage manager." He was not about to slow down, although he was nearly sixty years old. He needed to prove that he was still the strong, active man that he always had been.

Steinbeck remembered the trips he had made as a young man. He recalled living out of his bakery truck during the depression and voyaging to the Gulf of California with Ed Ricketts. He longed to travel freely once more.

Also, he wanted to get close to the American people again. Since becoming a famous man, Steinbeck felt cut off from the ordinary people he had once known so well. He wanted to explore the America of 1960.

He bought a pickup truck with a camper top and outfitted the vehicle with a stove, furniture, and supplies. He called the truck Rocinante, after the horse ridden by Don Quixote, another knight from literature. He told Elizabeth Otis that he planned to drive across the United States and back, to be "a wandering car and eye." He would travel anonymously with Elaine's poodle, Charley, for company. He would write a book about his adventures.

Just after Labor Day, when Steinbeck was ready to drive off in Rocinante, a hurricane struck Long Island. The aging author's strength and stamina had an unexpected test.

Ninety-five-mile-an-hour winds battered the Steinbecks' little bluff. John and Charley waited out the storm with Elaine, inside their cottage. They watched from a window as trees snapped and rising water covered their pier. And then John saw that his boat, the *Fayre Eleyne*, was in trouble. Two other boats had pulled free from their moorings and were crashing against its sides. The wind was pushing John's craft into a heavy oaken pile.

Afraid that he would see his beloved boat smashed to bits, John raced out of the house. Ignoring the rain and wind, he worked his way to the end of the pier, which was now under four feet of water. He climbed aboard the *Fayre Eleyne*, started its engine, hoisted up the anchor, and then piloted the boat out onto the rough water, one hundred yards from shore. He let down the anchor and felt it dig into the floor of the bay. "The *Fayre Eleyne* straightened and raised her bow and seemed to sigh with relief," he noted, and he gave a sigh of his own.

John's only problem now was getting back to shore. When he saw a large branch float past, he dived into the water as if he were a much younger man. He grabbed the limb and floated in with it. Soon, Elaine and a neighbor were anxiously pulling him onto the land.

The storm passed, and the sky cleared. John Steinbeck revved up the motor in Rocinante and left to tour America. He went north to Maine,

John Steinbeck and Charley.

where he drank beer with French Canadian farm workers. The Canadians crossed the U.S. border every fall to work in the potato harvest. In northern Michigan, Steinbeck went fishing with a groundskeeper he befriended. The man at first had tried to kick Steinbeck off the land where he had parked Rocinante for the night!

Steinbeck ate dinner with families living in trailer parks. He had a "love affair" with Montana, a state that awed him with its broad, open landscapes and imposing mountains.

In California, Steinbeck returned to Salinas and to Cannery Row. He felt like a ghost from the past. He wrote, "I remember Salinas, the town of my birth, when it proudly announced four thousand citizens. Now it is eighty thousand and leaping pell mell on in a mathematical progression—a hundred thousand in three years and perhaps two hundred thousand in ten, with no end in sight." Cannery Row had become a tourist attraction: "The canneries which once put up a sickening stench are gone, their places filled with restaurants, antique shops and the like."

Steinbeck and Charley followed the route of the Dust Bowl migrants in reverse. They went through the farming regions around Fresno and Bakersfield, across the Mojave Desert, Arizona, and New Mexico, and into Texas. After enjoying a Thanksgiving feast on a Texas ranch, they headed for New Orleans.

Louisiana's largest city had been in the news lately, due to a cruel daily ritual that took place outside one of its schools. In the mornings, a group of white women lined up to shout insults and obscenities at children attending a newly desegregated school. The women were known as the Cheerleaders, and a crowd gathered each morning to watch the show they put on.

John Steinbeck joined the crowd on a bright, chilly morning. He saw armed U.S. marshals keeping people back from the entrance to the school. The marshals had come to New Orleans to enforce integration. In 1954, the Supreme Court had ruled that segregated public schools, then prevalent in the South, violated the rights guaranteed by the

Constitution. However, in spite of the Supreme Court ruling, southern communities resisted letting black students into their all-white schools.

Steinbeck watched the marshals escort a tiny black girl to school. "The little girl did not look at the howling crowd but from the side the whites of her eyes showed like those of a frightened fawn," he observed. As the Cheerleaders taunted and jeered, the marshals led the child toward the school building.

The shouting grew louder when a man brought his white child to school. To these hate-filled women, any parent who allowed his son or daughter to learn alongside African Americans was a traitor to the cause of segregation. "The yelling was not in a chorus," Steinbeck reported. "Each took a turn and at the end of each the crowd broke into howls and roars and whistles of applause."

The author was sickened by the display of "crazy actors playing to a crazy audience." He admired Charley's ability to accept others regardless of their appearance. "It would be difficult to explain to a dog the good and moral purpose of a thousand humans gathered to curse one tiny human," he said.

John wrote letters to Elaine, telling her of his adventures. Sometimes he telephoned her. During one of those conversations, Elaine told her husband how much she enjoyed his letters. They reminded her of Robert Louis Stevenson's *Travels with a Donkey*. She thought of them as his Travels with Charley. "You've just given me my title," John told her.

In *Travels with Charley in Search of America*, which was published in 1962, Steinbeck chatted with his readers. He asked them to think of him "bowling along on some little road or pulled up behind a bridge, or cooking a big pot of lima beans and salt pork," as he talked about what he had seen.

Mass production and mass communication were making distant regions of the nation more and more alike. Steinbeck commented on the roadside restaurants where he ate, places with "great scallops of counters with simulated leather stools," all looking the same. In all of these eateries, "the food is oven-fresh, spotless and tasteless; untouched by human hands," he remarked. "It is almost as though the customers had no interest in what they ate as long as it had no character to embarrass them."

Vending machines were everywhere, selling soft drinks, nail files, cosmetics, medicines, hot soup, ice, and newspapers. The automation made life on the road convenient, but lonely. John startled some guests at a Seattle hotel by wishing them a good evening. He wrote, "It seemed to me that they looked at me for a place to insert a coin"!

Thanks to television and radio, regional accents were disappearing. Steinbeck had spent a lifetime listening to Americans speak, and this change made him sad. "For with local accent will disappear local tempo," he explained. "The idioms, the figures of speech that make the language rich and full of poetry of place and time must go. And in their place will be a national speech, wrapped and packaged, standard and tasteless."

Whatever the region or its manner of speech, Steinbeck expected to meet Americans with deep roots. Instead, he encountered a restless people, always eager to be someplace else. Driving near Toledo, Ohio, he said to Charley that perhaps this rootlessness is at the heart of American culture. "The pioneers, the immigrants who peopled the continent were the restless ones in Europe. The steady rooted ones stayed home and are still there. But every one of us, except the Negroes forced here as slaves, are descended from the restless ones, the way-ward ones who were not content to stay home."

John Steinbeck deplored the racism he saw on his trip, and he criticized the changes wrought by progress and time. Yet he carried home a positive image of the American people. He explained that in spite of America's geographic and cultural diversity, "we are a nation, a new breed. Americans are much more American than they are Northerners, Southerners, Westerners, or Easterners." He added, "California Chinese, Boston Irish, Wisconsin German, yes, and Alabama Negroes, have more in common than they have apart."

The knight and his squire—man and dog—ended their quest eleven weeks after leaving Sag Harbor. Steinbeck crossed the river into New York City and was driving down a crowded street when he pulled Rocinante over to the curb and started laughing. A police officer walked up and asked him what was wrong. "Officer," Steinbeck said, "I've driven this thing all over the country—mountains, plains, deserts. And now I'm back in my own town, where I live—and I'm lost."

John Steinbeck, Nobel Prize winner. (Courtesy of the Steinbeck Research Center, San Jose State University)

CHAPTER 10

The Old Tailor

On the morning of October 25, 1962, Elaine Steinbeck was frying bacon in the Sag Harbor cottage. John turned on the television to catch up on the news before breakfast. He was startled to hear the newscaster announce, "John Steinbeck has been awarded the Nobel Prize for Literature."

The Swedish Academy, which awards the prize each year, had selected Steinbeck over all the other writers in the world. The prize honored not one of his books, but all of them. He would receive the Nobel Prize in Stockholm, from King Gustav VI Adolph of Sweden.

The news came as a complete surprise. John had had no idea that he was being considered for the Nobel Prize. Elaine was so excited that she put her pan of sizzling bacon in the refrigerator!

For John Steinbeck, there was no way to avoid reporters' questions and cameras now. He held a press conference at the offices of The Viking Press in New York City. When the reporters asked how he felt about winning the prize, Steinbeck replied, "Wrapped and shellacked." The men and women of the press kept asking what he meant. Steinbeck explained that he felt like a cracked fishing pole that had been repaired with fishing line and shellac. But later he admitted that he had meant nothing by his answer. "I enjoyed it thoroughly," he added, "because everybody interpreted it differently, and all I was doing was having a little fun."

When a reporter asked him if he deserved the Nobel Prize, he responded humbly: "Frankly, no."

Some critics in America agreed. Just one day after the prize was announced, an editorial in the *New York Times* stated, "The award of the Nobel Prize for Literature to John Steinbeck will focus attention once again on a writer who, though still in full career, produced his major work more than two decades ago." This editorial writer and others were still waiting for Steinbeck to repeat what he had done in *The Grapes of Wrath*. Many Americans, however, took a new look at Steinbeck's stories and novels. Sales of his books soared, especially among young readers.

Europeans, in contrast, were united in their esteem for Steinbeck's achievements. At the award ceremony in Stockholm, on December 10, 1962, the secretary of the Swedish Academy spoke for Steinbeck's fans throughout the world. Secretary Anders Osterling said, "With your most distinctive works you have become a teacher of goodwill and charity, a defender of human values, which can well be said to correspond to the proper idea of the Nobel Prize."

And then John Steinbeck, the writer who had avoided public appearances for so long, stood before an audience of dignitaries to receive the greatest honor of his life. The man who for years had declined to give speeches now felt "impelled not to squeak like a grateful and apologetic mouse, but to roar like a lion," he said. He spoke about a writer's responsibility to address wrongs and to educate.

"A writer," said Steinbeck, "is charged with exposing our many grievous faults and failures, with dredging up to the light our dark and dangerous dreams, for the purpose of improvement.

"Furthermore, the writer is delegated to declare and to celebrate man's proven capacity for greatness of heart and spirit—for gallantry in defeat, for courage, compassion, and love. In the endless war against weakness and despair, these are the bright rally-flags of hope and of emulation."

In 1963, President John F. Kennedy invited Steinbeck to carry the

Steinbeck accepts the Nobel Prize from King Gustav VI Adolph of Sweden.

Wanting to "roar like a lion" after receiving the Nobel Prize, Steinbeck speaks about a writer's responsibility.

Autographing copies of his books for fans in Budapest, Hungary.

John Steinbeck, carrying a walking stick, and Elaine Steinbeck view the Berlin Wall.

bright rally-flags into the communist countries of Europe. Kennedy asked the Nobel Prize winner to serve as a cultural ambassador, to carry information about American literature behind the Iron Curtain. President Kennedy also recommended that John Steinbeck receive the Medal of Freedom, the nation's highest honor for civilians. The president wished to recognize Steinbeck's service to his country over the years.

John, Elaine, and a young playwright, Edward Albee, flew to the Soviet Union in the fall of 1963. The two American writers attended meetings and luncheons with Soviet authors. These were stuffy, official gatherings, sanctioned by the Soviet government. Steinbeck pressed the writers to speak openly about books and politics, but he had no luck. "Young wolves, show me your teeth," he challenged.

The Russian writer Bella Akhmadulina reminded Steinbeck that he was free to return to the United States, where people have the right to speak their minds. The others had to remain in the Soviet Union. They had to think of their safety and be careful about what they said.

Steinbeck also met secretly with college students in their dormitory rooms. At those meetings, away from the government's listening ear, everyone felt free to speak about literature and ideas.

The American cultural ambassadors visited Poland, Hungary, and Czechoslovakia. They traveled to Berlin, then a divided city. A wall of concrete and barbed wire separated East Berlin, part of communist East Germany, from West Berlin, belonging to democratic West Germany. The wall prevented East Berliners from escaping to the West. To Steinbeck, the Berlin Wall was an admission by the communists that their system of government had failed. "That's what this amounts to," he said, looking at the wall, "a failure in competition, a failure in everything."

President Kennedy was assassinated while the Steinbecks were in Poland. John and Elaine considered going home when they heard the tragic news. But John decided that finishing his mission in Europe would be the best way to honor the fallen president. He attended his meetings with Polish writers as scheduled.

President Johnson presents the Medal of Freedom to John Steinbeck on September 14, 1964.

And he later received the honor that Kennedy had wanted him to have. President Lyndon Johnson presented the Medal of Freedom to John Steinbeck on September 14, 1964.

Elaine Steinbeck and Lady Bird Johnson, the president's wife, had attended college together. They recently had renewed their friendship. The Johnsons invited the Steinbecks to stay at the White House from time to time. When Lyndon Johnson accepted the Democratic party's nomination for president in 1964, he delivered a speech that John Steinbeck had written.

Later life brought recognition and friends in high places, but it also brought loss. A month after Steinbeck was honored at the White House, his editor and friend for almost thirty years, Pascal Covici, died. John's sister Mary died of cancer at Christmastime.

A year later, the Steinbecks were in Ireland. Thinking of Mary, John walked alone on a seaside cliff. He looked out across the frigid Atlantic and watched the gulls coasting on the ocean breezes. He claimed that Mary had been with him on that cliff, and that he had talked with her.

Time was claiming friends and loved ones. Even Charley had grown old and died. Old values and customs seemed to be disappearing, too. John Steinbeck, remembering the past, was unhappy with what he saw.

Steinbeck had lived through two world wars. Twice, he had seen

At the home of Dook Sheffield, November 1964.

John and Elaine. (Courtesy of the Steinbeck Research Center, San Jose State University)

Americans unite in a spirit of patriotism to defeat an enemy on the battlefield and to support the war effort at home. He had done his part in World War II by reporting on the fighting in Europe. Now, young people were boldly protesting against the United States' involvement in a war in Southeast Asia.

Since the early 1960s, American troops had been helping the army of South Vietnam combat an invasion force from communist North Vietnam. Every year, the American presence in Vietnam had grown larger. President Kennedy had sent four hundred soldiers to Saigon, the capital of South Vietnam, in 1961. There were nearly 200,000 American combat personnel in Vietnam by the end of 1965.

The Vietnam War divided American society. Many people believed that the United States had no business meddling in a war between two factions in a small Asian country. They held marches and rallies, and called on the government to bring the U.S. forces home. To others, such a stance was unpatriotic. They considered it the duty of every American to support the efforts of the military.

John Steinbeck belonged to the second group. He understood that the war was complicated, with China and the Soviet Union aiding the Viet Cong, the communist fighting force. Also, he had witnessed life under communism, and he hated the repression he had seen.

Steinbeck viewed the protesters as spoiled children who did not want to give up their comfortable lives to go to war. He called the protesters "Vietnicks," and he felt shame at the sight of them. He dismissed them as a collection of "dirty clothes, dirty minds, sour smelling wastelings. . . ."

Steinbeck's attitude puzzled many of his admirers. They expected him to speak out against the war, as he had spoken out about issues in the past. Some wondered publicly whether the author's friendship with President Johnson had influenced his opinion. Johnson had steadily expanded the U.S. commitment in Vietnam.

The Russian poet Yevgeny Yevtushenko remembered Steinbeck's challenge to the writers in Moscow. Now, Yevtushenko chided in a poem, "John, you're an old wolf. / So show your teeth. . ."

In response, Steinbeck proposed to the poet that they go to Vietnam together. That way, they could see for themselves what was going on. The Soviet government denied Yevtushenko permission to make the trip, so Steinbeck went without him. He traveled as a reporter for *Newsday*.

John and Elaine Steinbeck flew to Saigon in December 1966. Elaine would explore the city while John took a look at the war. They got a taste of warfare even before their plane touched the ground. The pilot had to dive and swerve to avoid gunfire from nearby battles. The Steinbecks were met at the airport by their son John, now a grown man of twenty. Young John was in the army and stationed in Vietnam.

War protesters clash with military police in Washington, D.C., in October 1967.

Steinbeck, fifth from left, poses with American Green Berets in Vietnam.

During his six weeks in Vietnam, John Steinbeck saw and did as much as he could. He learned from the soldiers how to fire modern weapons and avoid enemy booby traps in the hot Asian jungle. He rode to battle sites in military helicopters, and he praised the pilots for their skill. "They ride their vehicles the way a man controls a fine, well-trained quarter horse," he wrote. "They weave along stream beds, rise like swallows to clear trees, they turn and twist and dip like swifts in the evening."

Steinbeck thrilled as his helicopter flew over steep mountains and cascading waterfalls. Then, suddenly, the aircraft would descend into a canyon to follow a stream. "You realize that the low green cover you saw from high up is a towering screaming jungle so dense that noonday light fails to reach the ground," Steinbeck noted. "The stream bed twists like a snake and we snake over it, now and then lofting like a tipped fly ball to miss an obstruction or cutting around a tree the way a good cow horse cuts out a single calf from a loose herd."

As in World War II, Steinbeck wanted to be part of the action. He rode in the lead helicopter during an army assault on the enemy. He moved through the jungle with Marines staging a ground attack. He thought that the hardworking, well-trained American forces were the opposite of the protesting "Vietnicks." He asked in *Newsday*, "Can you understand the quick glow of pride one feels in just belonging to the same species as these men?"

From Vietnam, the Steinbecks went to neighboring Thailand. Refugees from North Vietnam were pouring into that country, and among them were communist soldiers. And the war was creeping over the border of Laos, which was thought to be a neutral nation. American planes were even dropping bombs in Laos, a fact that was kept hidden from the public. John Steinbeck now saw that the war in Vietnam was highly complex, and that it could easily grow and spread. If that happened, the United States might never be able to win. No longer could he give unquestioning support to the U.S. war effort—but he continued to back the soldiers. He wrote, "If I could shorten this war by one hour

Steinbeck in Vietnam.

by going back to Vietnam, I would be on tonight's plane with a one-way ticket."

John and Elaine stopped in Hong Kong, a British dependency on the Chinese mainland, before heading home. They were out walking one day when they saw a man struggling to pull some heavy crates up a flight of steps with a hand truck. John gave the man a hand. But when he pulled at the load, he felt a sudden pain in his back. He had injured a disk, one of the cushions of tissue that separate the vertebrae. That injury marked a turning point in John Steinbeck's life. He would never be his old, active self again.

The Steinbecks returned to the United States in April 1967. By Memorial Day, John's back was so painful that he could hardly move. Doctors who examined him said that surgery would help. They hesitated to operate, though, because they had found his heart to be weak. (The heart condition may have caused Steinbeck's mysterious fainting spells in earlier years.) The back pain at last grew unbearable, and in late October, John Steinbeck entered the hospital.

A writer named Budd Schulberg went to see Steinbeck in his hospital room on the night before the operation. "With his craggy mountain of a face, his powerful chest, his sturdy body, he looked too big for that hospital bed," Schulberg recalled in his book *The Four Seasons of Success*.

Steinbeck talked to his visitor about how it felt to have spent a lifetime writing. "I'm like an old tailor," he explained. "Put a needle and thread in my hand and a piece of cloth and I begin to sew." Instead of a tailor's needle and thread, however, Steinbeck was used to holding a pencil. "My hands have to keep busy," he continued. "I have to hold a pencil in my fingers. I need to write some pages every day."

Life as a writer had been a long and eventful journey for John Steinbeck. Always searching for a story to tell, he had driven countless miles along America's farm roads and highways. He had explored Mexico's coastline and Europe's crumbling castles. He had shaken the hands of migrant workers, soldiers, presidents, and a king. He now wrote to Dook Sheffield, his oldest friend, that so much of the journey still lay ahead. He had never been to Africa. He wanted to visit the Watts Writers Workshop, a group of young writers in a poor Los Angeles community. His book about King Arthur waited to be finished.

The operation was a success, and by December Steinbeck felt well enough to vacation in the Virgin Islands. But soon, his heart gave him trouble. He was back in the hospital by summer, after spells of heart failure left him gasping for breath.

John Steinbeck knew he was dying. He asked to go to Sag Harbor, to see the scenery he loved. When he felt up to it, he walked on the bluff with Angel, a white bull terrier that was the last dog he owned. He was glad to see friends when they came to visit.

With November's chill, John's health worsened. Elaine moved him to their Manhattan home, to be close to his doctors. He died peacefully at 5:30 in the afternoon on December 20, 1968, with Elaine lying at his side. He was sixty-six years old.

John Steinbeck had asked for a simple funeral with no flowers or long speeches. A small group of his loved ones and friends gathered in a New York church for a twenty-minute service. They listened to Henry Fonda, the actor who had played Tom Joad in the film *The Grapes of Wrath*, read some of Steinbeck's favorite poems.

Fonda read "Ulysses," by Alfred, Lord Tennyson. Ulysses, also called Odysseus, was a great sea captain in ancient Greek lore. Tennyson portrayed him as an aging man who was still ready for new voyages and experiences, as Steinbeck had been:

> *I cannot rest from travel; I will drink*
> *Life to the lees. All time I have enjoyed*
> *Greatly, have suffered greatly, both with those*
> *That love me, and alone . . .*

After the funeral service, Elaine embraced the other mourners outside the church. She asked them to "remember him. Remember him!"

Elaine and Thom carried John's ashes to California on Christmas

John Steinbeck, 1902–1968. (Courtesy of the Steinbeck Research Center, San Jose State University)

Eve. A few days later, the Steinbeck family gathered for a private service in Pacific Grove. From a cliff where John had played with Mary so many years before, a priest cast John's ashes into the ocean.

The world has remembered John Steinbeck in the decades following his death. Young people especially continue to enjoy his writings. *Tortilla Flat, Of Mice and Men, Cannery Row*—a number of Steinbeck's books are considered American classics. Since his most important book, *The Grapes of Wrath*, was published, in 1939, four and one-half million copies have been sold in the United States. Fourteen million, in a variety of languages, have been sold throughout the world. Americans now buy 100,000 copies of the epic depression novel every year.

The contemporary novelist William Kennedy wrote about *The Grapes of Wrath* in 1989, on the fiftieth anniversary of its publication. In an article for the *New York Times Book Review*, Kennedy remarked that the issues Steinbeck raised during the depression are still important today. The wandering, desperate Joads reminded him of the homeless men and women living in America's cities, "people at the bottom of the world, bereft and drifting outcasts in a hostile society." Kennedy asked himself whether, after fifty years, the book stands up. "It does indeed," he concluded. "It stands tall."

In 1939, a university student who was doing research on Steinbeck and his books sent the author a questionnaire. The student asked him about his life and about the characters he had created. She also asked him to explain his philosophy. Steinbeck replied that no deep philosophical idea formed the basis of his work. "I don't like people to be hurt or hungry or unnecessarily sad," he wrote. "It's just about as simple as that."

Books by John Steinbeck

FICTION

Cup of Gold. New York: Robert M. McBride and Company, 1929.

The Pastures of Heaven. New York: Brewer, Warren and Putnam, 1932.

To a God Unknown. New York: Robert O. Ballou, 1933.

Tortilla Flat. New York: Covici-Friede, 1935.

In Dubious Battle. New York: Covici-Friede, 1936.

Of Mice and Men. New York: Covici-Friede, 1937.

The Red Pony. New York: The Viking Press, 1937.

The Long Valley. New York: The Viking Press, 1938.

The Grapes of Wrath. New York: The Viking Press, 1939.

The Forgotten Village. New York: The Viking Press, 1941.

The Moon Is Down. New York: The Viking Press, 1942.

Cannery Row. New York: The Viking Press, 1945.

The Wayward Bus. New York: The Viking Press, 1947.

The Pearl. New York: The Viking Press, 1947.

Burning Bright. New York: The Viking Press, 1950.

East of Eden. New York: The Viking Press, 1952.

Sweet Thursday. New York: The Viking Press, 1954.

The Short Reign of Pippin IV: A Fabrication. New York: The Viking Press, 1957.

The Winter of Our Discontent. New York: The Viking Press, 1961.

The Acts of King Arthur and His Noble Knights. New York: Farrar, Straus and Giroux, 1976. (Steinbeck's unfinished book was published after his death.)

NONFICTION

The Sea of Cortez: A Leisurely Journal of Travel and Research (with Edward F. Ricketts). New York: The Viking Press, 1941.

Bombs Away: The Story of a Bomber Team. New York: The Viking Press, 1942.

A Russian Journal (with photographs by Robert Capa). New York: The Viking Press, 1948.

The Log from the Sea of Cortez. New York: The Viking Press, 1951. (Steinbeck's account of the voyage of the *Western Flyer* from the earlier book *The Sea of Cortez*; contains the essay "About Ed Ricketts".)

Once There Was a War. New York: The Viking Press, 1958. (Steinbeck's wartime articles for the *Herald Tribune*.)

Travels with Charley in Search of America. New York: The Viking Press, 1962.

America and Americans. New York: The Viking Press, 1966.

Journal of a Novel: The East of Eden *Letters.* New York: The Viking Press, 1969.

The Harvest Gypsies. Berkeley, Cal.: Heyday Books, 1988. (Steinbeck's 1936 articles on the Dust Bowl migrants for the *San Francisco News*.)

Selected Bibliography

Benson, Jackson J., ed. *The Short Novels of John Steinbeck: Critical Essays with a Checklist to Steinbeck Criticism.* Durham, N.C.: Duke University Press, 1990.

———. *The True Adventures of John Steinbeck, Writer.* New York: The Viking Press, 1984.

Bidwell, Martin. "John Steinbeck: An Impression." *Prairie Schooner,* Spring 1938.

Bloom, Harold, ed. *Modern Critical Views: John Steinbeck.* New York: Chelsea House Publishers, 1987.

Davis, Robert Murray, ed. *Steinbeck: A Collection of Critical Essays.* Englewood Cliffs, N.J.: Prentice-Hall, Inc., 1972.

Fensch, Thomas, ed. *Conversations with John Steinbeck.* Jackson, Miss.: University Press of Mississippi, 1988.

French, Warren. *John Steinbeck.* Boston: Twayne Publishers, 1975.

Gray, James. *John Steinbeck.* Minneapolis: University of Minnesota Press, 1971.

Gregory, James N. *American Exodus: The Dust Bowl Migration and Okie Culture in California.* New York: Oxford University Press, 1989.

Kennedy, William. " 'My Work Is No Good.' " *The New York Times Book Review,* April 9, 1989.

Lisca, Peter. *John Steinbeck: Nature and Myth.* New York: Thomas Y. Crowell, 1978.

McWilliams, Carey. *Factories in the Field: The Story of Migratory Farm Labor in California*. N.p.: Archon Books, 1969.

Meister, Dick, and Anne Loftis. *A Long Time Coming: The Struggle to Unionize America's Farm Workers*. New York: Macmillan, 1977.

Steinbeck, Elaine, and Robert Wallsten, eds. *Steinbeck: A Life in Letters*. New York: Penguin Books, 1975.

Steinbeck, John. "A Primer on the 30's." *Esquire*, June 1960.

———. "Always Something to Do in Salinas." *Holiday*, June 1955.

———. "Autobiography: Making of a New Yorker." *The New York Times Magazine, Part II*, February 1, 1953.

———. "I Go Back to Ireland." *Collier's*, January 31, 1953.

———. "The Soul and Guts of France." *Collier's*, August 30, 1952.

———. "The Trial of Arthur Miller." *Esquire*, June 1957.

———. *Working Days: The Journals of* The Grapes of Wrath. Robert De Mott, ed. New York: The Viking Press, 1989.

Watkins, T. H. *The Great Depression: America in the 1930s*. Boston: Little, Brown, 1993.

Acknowledgments and Picture Credits

I wish to thank all of the librarians and scholars who provided help and suggestions during the preparation of this book, especially Mary Jean S. Gamble, Steinbeck librarian, the John Steinbeck Library, Salinas, California; Susan Shillinglaw, director of the Steinbeck Research Center, San Jose State University, San Jose, California; Linda Long, public services librarian, Stanford University, Stanford, California; and Dianne Nilsen of the Center for Creative Photography, the University of Arizona, Tucson, Arizona.

Dorothea Lange for the Farm Security Administration, The Library of Congress: x, 2, 28, 59, 61, 70, 73, 74, 75, 79, 80, 83

Arthur Rothstein for the Farm Security Administration, The Library of Congress: 71, 72, 76, 78

The Library of Congress: 14, 31, 32, 35, 38, 42, 43, 45, 58, 97, 101, 144

Still photo, page 87, from "The Grapes of Wrath" © 1940, Twentieth Century Fox Film Corporation. All rights reserved.

Photograph by Sonya Noskowiak, copyright Arthur Noskowiak, Department of Special Collections, Stanford University Libraries: 5

Department of Special Collections, Stanford University Libraries: 24, 46

Courtesy of the Steinbeck Research Center, San Jose State University: ii, 65, 95, 103, 104, 105, 108, 134, 142, 150

Mrs. E. G. Ainsworth, Courtesy of the Steinbeck Archives of the Salinas Public Library, Salinas, California: 8, 11, 12, 13, 18, 115, 116, 137, 147

Courtesy of the Steinbeck Archives of the Salinas Public Library, Salinas, California: 16, 19, 56, 118

California History Room, California State Library, Courtesy of the Steinbeck Archives of the Salinas Public Library, Salinas, California: 10, 22

Valley Guild, Courtesy of the Steinbeck Archives of the Salinas Public Library, Salinas, California: 21, 138

Bill Emery, Steinbeck Library, Salinas, California: 27

James Speck, Courtesy of the Steinbeck Archives of the Salinas Public Library, Salinas, California: 49

Richard Albee, Courtesy of the Steinbeck Archives of the Salinas Public Library, Salinas, California: 63

Elaine Steinbeck, Courtesy of the Steinbeck Archives of the Salinas Public Library, Salinas, California: 138, 145

Western History Collections, University of Oklahoma Library: 68

John Steinbeck Collection (#6239), Clifton Waller Barrett Library, Special Collections Department, University of Virginia Library: 84

The National Archives: 95

Copyright the Estate of Hans Namuth, Collection of the Center for Creative Photography, the University of Arizona: 129

UPI/The Bettmann Archive: 126

Cecil Stoughton, Lyndon B. Johnson Library Collection: 140

Carlton Sheffield, Courtesy of the Steinbeck Archives of the Salinas Public Library, Salinas, California: 141

Courtesy of Culver Pictures, Inc.: 120

Index

Numbers in *italics* indicate illustrations.

About the Author

"When I was in junior high and ready to read adult books, one of the first authors I came to know and enjoy was John Steinbeck," says Catherine Reef. "Steinbeck appeals to young readers because he shows that it is possible to enter adulthood yet never lose the idealism, courage, and natural humor of youth."

Catherine Reef is the author of more than twenty nonfiction books for young people, most recently *Walt Whitman*. She received her B.A. in English from Washington State University, and lives in Montgomery Village, Maryland, with her husband, her teenage son, their dog, and several tanks of tropical fish.